GCSE Music Listening Tests

Andrew S. Coxon and Philip Taylor

R·
Rhinegold Education

239–241 Shaftesbury Avenue
London WC2H 8TF
Telephone: 020 7333 1720
Fax: 020 7333 1765

www.rhinegold.co.uk

Music Study Guides

GCSE, AS and A2 Music Study Guides (AQA, Edexcel and OCR)
GCSE, AS and A2 Music Listening Tests (AQA, Edexcel and OCR)
GCSE Music Study Guide (WJEC)
GCSE Music Listening Tests (WJEC)
AS/A2 Music Technology Study Guide (Edexcel)
AS/A2 Music Technology Listening Tests (Edexcel)
Revision Guides for GCSE (AQA, Edexcel and OCR), AS and A2 Music (Edexcel)

Also available from Rhinegold Education

Key Stage 3 Listening Tests: Book 1 and Book 2
AS and A2 Music Harmony Workbooks
GCSE and AS Music Composition Workbooks
GCSE and AS Music Literacy Workbooks
Romanticism in Focus, Baroque Music in Focus, Film Music in Focus,
Modernism in Focus, *The Immaculate Collection* in Focus, *Who's Next* in Focus,
Batman in Focus, *Goldfinger* in Focus, Musicals in Focus,
Music Technology from Scratch

Rhinegold also publishes Choir & Organ, Classical Music, Classroom Music, Early Music Today,
International Piano, Music Teacher, Muso, Opera Now, Piano, The Singer, Teaching Drama,
British and International Music Yearbook, British Performing Arts Yearbook, British Music Education Yearbook,
World Conservatoires, Rhinegold Dictionary of Music in Sound

Other Rhinegold Study Guides

Rhinegold publishes resources for candidates studying Drama and Theatre Studies.

First published 2010 in Great Britain by
Rhinegold Education
239–241 Shaftesbury Avenue
London WC2H 8TF
Telephone: 020 7333 1720
Fax: 020 7333 1765
www.rhinegold.co.uk

© Rhinegold Publishing Ltd 2010

All rights reserved. No part of this publication may be reproduced, stored in a retrieval system,
or transmitted in any form or by any means, electronic, mechanical, photocopying, recording or otherwise,
without the prior permission of Rhinegold Publishing Ltd.

The title is excluded from any licence issued by the Copyright Licensing Agency,
or other Reproduction Rights Organisation.

Rhinegold Publishing Ltd has used its best efforts in preparing this guide. It does not assume,
and hereby disclaims, any liability to any party, for loss or damage caused by errors or omissions in the guide,
whether such errors or omissions result from negligence, accident or other cause.

You should always check the current requirements of the examination, since these may change.
Copies of the AQA specification may be obtained from
Publications Department, AQA, Devas Street, Manchester M15 6EX
Telephone 0161 953 1180 Fax 0161 273 7572. See also the AQA website at www.aqa.org.uk

---

AQA GCSE Music Listening Tests
British Library Cataloguing in Publication Data.
A catalogue record for this book is available from the British Library.
ISBN 978-1-906178-89-5
Printed in England by Halstan & Co Ltd, Amersham, Bucks.

CONTENTS

INTRODUCTION	5
CLASSROOM ACTIVITIES	
RHYTHM & METRE	16
TEXTURE	18
MELODY	21
THE WESTERN CLASSICAL TRADITION	24
POPULAR MUSIC OF THE 20TH AND 21ST CENTURIES	50
WORLD MUSIC	71
MOCK LISTENING EXAMINATIONS	90
GLOSSARY	92

THE AUTHORS

Andrew S. Coxon is a practising classroom music teacher with 40 years' experience, currently teaching part-time at the Nelson Thomlinson School, Wigton, still covering music from Year 7 to A level. Until taking retirement from full-time teaching, he had been Head of Department in three secondary schools, most notably West Denton High School in Newcastle. In all, he was involved in annual musical productions and ran a wide range of instrumental and vocal groups. He has been involved in examination work with one of the major examining boards for 36 years and has held senior posts at GCSE and A level for some time. Examining work includes examined assessment and moderation of coursework. He recently co-authored two student books for new music specifications, one for GCSE, the other for AS/A2. He is an experienced composer and arranger, actively making music in a variety of ways, inside and outside school.

Philip Taylor is a freelance teacher, examiner and pianist. He has been a classroom music teacher for more than 20 years, most recently as director of music at Rishworth School, Yorkshire. Since leaving full-time teaching, he has taught music education and keyboard skills at Huddersfield University. He is a repetiteur and animateur for the education wing of Opera North, bringing the world of opera to young people around the north of England. He has been an examiner since 1985, and a senior examiner since 1996. Philip is also the author of Rhinegold's *AQA AS/A2 Music Listening Tests* (second edition) (Rhinegold, 2008).

THE EDITORS

Adrian Horsewood, Harriet Power, Katherine Smith, Richard Gumbley.

THE CONSULTANT

Chris Cook, Faculty Leader for Performing Arts, Temple Moor High School Science College.

AUDIO TRACKS

Please note that there is no CD to accompany this book. All the tracks for these tests are available to download from iTunes as one album or 'iMix'. To purchase and download the iMix, please go to the *AQA GCSE Music Listening Tests* (second edition) page at www.listeningtests.co.uk, where you will find a direct link to the iTunes store.

On the same webpage you will find a PDF entitled 'Rhinegold Education Listening Tests instructions', which provides help on using iTunes to play the tracks for these tests, as well as advice on alternative sources to iTunes for finding or downloading the tracks.

TEACHER'S GUIDE

Answers to all of the questions and a full track listing are given in the accompanying *Teacher's Guide* (RHG164), available from Rhinegold Education. Please note that all our books are now distributed by Music Sales: if you wish to buy online, you will be directed from our website through to musicroom.com. Alternatively, please call 01284 725 725 (01284 773 666 for schools).

COPYRIGHT

'The Farmer and the Cowman'. Words and Music by Oscar Hammerstein II and Richard Rodgers © 1943. Reproduced by permission of EMI Music Publishing Ltd, London W8 5SW.

'Golden Brown'. Words & Music by Jet Black, Jean-Jacques Burnel, Hugh Cornwell and David Greenfield © 1981 Plumbshaft Limited/Complete Music Limited (75%)/ EMI Music Publishing Limited (25%). All rights reserved. International copyright secured. Used by permission of Music Sales Ltd.

'Thank You for the Music'. By permission of Bocu Music Ltd.

'War In A Babylon'. Words & Music by Perry Lee Scratch and Romeo Max © Universal/Island Music Ltd. All rights reserved. International copyright secured. Used by permission of Music Sales Ltd.

'Castle on a Cloud'. Music by Claude-Michel Schönberg. Original lyrics by Alain Boublil & Jean-Marc Natel. English lyrics by Herbert Kretzmer. © (music & lyrics) 1980 Editions Musicales Alain Boublil. English lyrics © 1985 Alain Boublil Music Ltd (ASCAP). All rights reserved. International copyright secured. Used by permission of Music Sales Ltd.

'Schindler's List'. Music by John Williams. © 1993 Universal/MCA Music Ltd. obo USI B Music Publ. All rights reserved. International copyright secured. Used by permission of Music Sales Ltd.

INTRODUCTION

Welcome to Rhinegold's **AQA GCSE Music Listening Tests**. This book will help you to prepare for the **Listening to and Appraising Music** paper which forms part of the assessment for the new GCSE syllabus.

The new AQA GCSE Music specification contains units which cover the three Assessment Objectives (AOs):

- AO1 Performing skills: performing/realising music with technical control, expression and interpretation
- AO2 Composing skills: creating and developing musical ideas with technical control and coherence
- AO3 Listening and appraising skills: analysing and evaluating music using musical terminology.

The GCSE Music course is assessed through your responses in four different units. The **Listening to and Appraising Music** test is normally taken as part of your final examinations at GCSE (that is, in June of your final year) – it lasts for an hour and is worth 20% of the final total of marks.

The other three units can be done at any time during the two-year course and your teacher will decide on the best way of spreading these out across the course. All have to be completed by early in May of the second year of your GCSE course.

The Listening to and Appraising Music test is administered by a CD containing musical excerpts, with your answers written into an examination booklet. The aim of this book is to give examples of some of the different types of questions you will encounter, to point out the most common challenges and difficulties within them and to provide valuable practice at examination-style questions.

> The structure of the AQA GCSE Music examination is discussed in more detail in the AQA GCSE Music Study Guide by Richard Knight (Rhinegold, 2009).

HOW TO USE THIS BOOK

There is a range of ways in which the questions in this book can be used:

- Your teacher could base a lesson on one of the questions, discussing the various terms, references and musical elements which are the focus of the individual parts of the question. Members of the group could suggest other ways in which they have used or encountered the various references – such as a rhythmic figure, a cadence, a modulation, a specific instrumental/vocal timbre, a particular ensemble and so on. Ideas could be shared on how to recognise the different features within the excerpt.
- A question could be set for homework or extension work.
- An individual question could be used to improve examination techniques and the ability to respond to the questions within the correct number of playings. Where this is done, time should be allowed to read through the question and then the excerpt should be played the given number of times, with pauses of about 20–30 seconds in between.
- All questions are accompanied by answers, which are available in a separate guide for your teacher. When you have completed the question your teacher

will check your answers against what we have suggested but also, where a range of answers is possible, talk about other responses which would have gained credit. Remember that any Mark Scheme is considered to be a working document as it is always possible that there will be other valid ways of responding to a question than those listed. If you are in any doubt as to whether or not your own answer deserves credit, discuss this with your teacher.

- At the end of the questions, on page 90, suggestions will be made as to how to select combinations of questions to produce a balanced paper which will add up to a total of 80 marks, thus matching the total which will be awarded in the AQA Listening to and Appraising Paper.

- A small group of questions could be set as a 'mini' mock examination, perhaps four or five. These should cover the different types of questions which will be encountered – including one with notation where missing notes of a melody have to be added, one where a rhythm is to be recognised, one without any musical notation at all and one which includes some extended writing. Three minutes should be allowed for reading through the questions and a pause of about 1 minute between each question. As excerpts are quite short and questions relatively few, the total time for four to five questions will range from 20 to 25 minutes.

THE GCSE EXAMINATION

The AQA specification is built around five Areas of Study (AoS), each of which contains two elements of music:

- AoS1   Rhythm and Metre
- AoS2   Harmony and Tonality
- AoS3   Texture and Melody
- AoS4   Timbre and Dynamics
- AoS5   Structure and Form

Each of these AoS is further defined on pages 8–9 of the specification and further clarification is given below.

Your teacher will give examples of how different composers have used these elements as the building blocks of their music. Excerpts will be chosen from the three **Strands of Learning** as given on page 10 of the specification, which are:

- The Western Classical Tradition
- Popular Music of the 20th and 21st centuries
- World Music

The AQA GCSE Music specification can be downloaded from the AQA website, www.aqa.org.uk

Although suggestions are given within the specification for particular listening areas within these strands, your teacher is free to choose any music which will demonstrate the use of, for example, rhythm, tonality, texture and so on or combinations of these.

THE LISTENING EXAMINATION

The total number of marks on this paper is 80 and this will be worth 20% of your final GCSE mark. Each question will include boxes to enable you to tick off the different playings so you know how many you have heard and how many more are to come. The number of marks for each subsection will be given, as will the total for the question.

You will have three minutes before the excerpts are played to read through the questions. There will be pauses of about 15–20 seconds between each playing and longer pauses before each new question begins.

There will be a range of questions, some of which will include two or three different excerpts. The number of individual questions for each excerpt is likely to range from two to five. The types of questions will include:

- Questions with no musical notation
- Questions with a selection of pitch outlines from which the correct one is to be identified
- Questions with a range of rhythms from which the correct one is to be identified
- Questions with a score where the missing notes of a melody have to be added; in the majority of cases, the rhythm of the missing melody will be given
- Questions which include some sort of grid outlining bar numbers
- Open-ended questions
- Questions where two versions of the same music are to be compared.

However, remember that, while the questions based on an excerpt will probably refer to two or more different Elements of Music, each individual sub-question – (a), (b), (c), etc. – will focus on a single Element. Examples follow for each of the Areas of Study and exercises can be found in the 'Classroom Activities' chapter.

AoS1: Rhythm and Metre

What is the time signature of the following excerpt?

(1 mark)

> You should decide first if the pulse (or beat) of the music divides into two or three. If it is two, you should next decide whether the beat divides into groups of two quavers or three. If both answers are 'two', then a range of answers will usually be permitted, including 2/4, 4/4 or common time – C – and 2/2 or split common time – ₵.
>
> If it is two but the quavers are grouped in threes, then the excerpt is in compound time or 6/8.
>
> If you feel that there are three beats in a bar, then a time signature of 3/4 should be written.
>
> You should listen to a wide range of music and try to work out the time signature; if necessary, practise in groups with different rhythms.

Which of the following rhythms can be heard on the snare drum at the beginning of this excerpt? *Tick your answer.*

(1 mark)

> As part of your preparation for this type of question, work out the different rhythms in your head and also look for similarities and differences. For example, in the four patterns above, (i) and (iv) start with two equal quavers but the pattern on the second beat is different – look carefully and work out the change in rhythm; (ii) and (iii) start with the same pattern twice, but (ii) is – taa ta-te taa ta-te – while (iii) is ta-te taa ta-te taa.

AoS2: Harmony and Tonality

Name or describe the cadence at the end of this excerpt.

(2 marks)

Four cadences are listed in the specification. Given the wording of this question, you have a choice as to how you answer: you can name the cadence as either **perfect, plagal, imperfect** or **interrupted** (this will gain you 2 marks if you give the correct answer) or you can name the chords used. For example, for a perfect cadence, you could write V–I or dominant to tonic: in this case, you are given one mark for each correct chord.

Which of the following best describes the tonality of this excerpt?
Circle your answer.

        atonal   major   minor   modal

(1 mark)

Remember:

- atonal music will sound as if it is not in any key at all
- music in a major key tends to sound bright and cheerful (though there are examples of tragic music in a major key, such as the music for Question 8)
- music in a minor key is often associated with sadder, more serious or more formal occasions (though there are examples of lively music written in a minor key, such as the Badinerie by J. S. Bach)
- modal music can often be recognised because there is no 'leading note', i.e. no semitone between the seventh and eighth notes of the scale.

AoS3: Texture and Melody

Describe the texture of this excerpt.

(1 mark)

You need to bear in mind the different types of texture identified in the syllabus and then choose the one which best suits the excerpt you are being played.
You can prepare for this type of question by listening to music which reflects the different textures mentioned.

INTRODUCTION

On the score, fill in the missing notes in bars 3 and 4, using the given rhythm.

(6 marks)

For this example question, this is the correct answer:

One mark awarded per correct pitch.

This type of question tests your ability to hear the way in which a short melody moves and then to write the notes onto the stave. Being able to use musical notation or staff notation is a requirement of the specification and this is one way in which both that knowledge and your ability to hear different pitches can be tested.

In this type of question, always use the last note **before** the notes you have to fill in and the note which comes **after** the last note you will add as reference points for pitch. The excerpt is likely to be played four times to give you plenty of opportunity to work out the correct pitches. Make sure that you write them clearly so that there cannot be any doubt whether your notes are in a space or on a line: if it isn't clear, you will not get the mark.

In this case, the first note you add is on the **same pitch** (A) as the last written note and the last note you will add is an E, the **same pitch** as the written note which follows. Using this information from the score can help you check the notes you have added in and listen again if necessary.

Notice also that, in this case, all the notes move by step from one note to the next: this might not always be the case, but there will never be any big leaps. If you think the notes haven't moved by step, sing from one to the next *in your head* counting the steps. For example, if the notes are a third apart, you would think C–D–E (or whatever the three notes would be), singing the three pitches in your head and, if necessary, don't be ashamed to use your fingers to count!

AoS4: Timbre and Dynamics

What musical term best describes the dynamic at the beginning of this excerpt?

(1 mark)

To answer this, you can use Italian terms such as forte or piano; you can use their abbreviations – *f* or *p*; or you can simply describe the dynamic using English words – loud or quiet. Note that, in this case, it is the dynamic level **at the beginning of the excerpt** that is the focus of the question.

In some cases, you might be asked specifically to give the Italian term or you might be asked to choose from a list of dynamics using Italian terms. Read the question carefully before answering.

Name the melody instrument heard at the beginning of this excerpt.

(1 mark)

This tests your ability to recognise a particular instrumental timbre and you should practise by listening to a wide range of music and trying to identify the different instruments involved. Notice that it is focused on an instrument that can play different pitches so ignore any unpitched percussion instruments you might hear.

A question might also be set asking you to identify a family or group (ensemble) of instruments or even a playing/performance technique (such as pizzicato/plucking the strings or *con sordino*/with a mute).

AoS5: Structure and Form

Which of the following best fits the structure of this excerpt? *Circle your answer.*

   AABA   **AABB**   **ABCA**   **ABCD**

(1 mark)

For this type of question, listen to the excerpt and try to recognise when a phrase or melody returns. If there are contrasting sections, where do they come? Use any preparation time to note the similarities and differences between the patterns.

With the four patterns given above, two start with the first section (Section **A**) coming twice, the other two start with Section **A** once followed by a contrast (Section **B**). If you hear two different sections at the beginning, you then have to decide if, after a third new section (**C**), the music goes back to the start (Section **A**) or adds in yet another new section (**D**).

Start by deciding which of these patterns is correct up to the first two letters and then you can limit your choice to two options rather than four.

Which of the following terms best describes the form of this excerpt?
Circle your answer.

binary   **rondo**   **strophic**   **ternary**

(1 mark)

Each of these forms is listed in the specification and you need to become familiar with what each means and the differences between them: this is done through careful listening to a wide range of music under guidance and explanation from your teacher.

LISTENING-EXAMINATION TECHNIQUE

There are a range of 'Do's and 'Don't's when tackling a listening examination:

- **Do** look carefully at the mark allocation for each part of a question. This will tell you just how much detail is needed: for example, if there are two marks, then you will need to give two separate pieces of information to gain both marks. A good example of this is when you are asked to name a melodic interval: where this attracts two marks, your answer will need to be, for example, not just a 3rd but a **major** or **minor** 3rd.

  However, if a question about a cadence is worth 2 marks, it is likely to have asked you to 'Name or describe' the cadence. In this case, the name of the cadence (e.g. 'perfect', 'plagal') will be awarded 2 marks, as will 'V–I' or 'dominant–tonic'.

- **Do** look carefully at the options given in a multiple-choice question: work out just what it is that you will have to listen for in order to be able to determine the correct answer.
- **Do** read the question carefully and answer exactly what you are asked. For example, a question might ask you to comment on **timbre** and **texture** as used in a particular excerpt: make sure you focus on these two elements alone as any comments on the other elements will be ignored as irrelevant.
- **Do** learn to use your 'inner ear': if you are asked to choose between different rhythms or different melodic outlines, try to work out what they sound like **in your head** and spot where the differences occur.
- **Do** remember that each Element of Music has its own vocabulary and make sure you understand any musical terms that appear in the specification, including Italian terms for dynamics and tempo.
- **Do** remember that each question will focus on a particular element and you will be able to tell exactly which it is from the wording of the question (refer to the examples given above).
- **Do** remember that each question is linked to what you can actually **hear** in the excerpt.

- **Don't** waste the three minutes' reading time at the start. Look through the paper carefully and, especially, be ready for the first question: getting off to a good start will give you confidence.
- **Don't** dwell on a question you feel unsure about: put it behind you and resolve to do well on the next one.
- **Don't** give a choice of answers if you are asked for a single fact and only one mark is allocated: the examiner cannot accept this and will mark your answer as incorrect. It is not for the examiner to select the correct answer: you must do this yourself by giving only a single response.
- **Don't** leave an answer blank: try to have a well-informed guess within the element which forms the focus of the question. If necessary, write a note for yourself and refer back in the time after the final playing of the last excerpt.

LISTENING

During the two-year GCSE course, your teacher will play a lot of music from different periods, for different ensembles, in different styles and by many different composers. A lot of it will be new to you: always give the music a chance! You will be surprised just how much music is familiar to you through advertisements, in films, as theme tunes to programmes and, increasingly, as part of the soundtrack to computer games. It is likely that you will hear many pieces of music which you will find appealing and might even lead you to research other pieces by the same composer, singer, group and so on.

If you are an instrumentalist or a singer, explore the wider repertoire of composers whose music you come across. For example, if you are preparing for a grade examination, whether with the Associated Board of the Royal Schools of Music (ABRSM), Trinity Guildhall or Rock School, be prepared to find other pieces by the composers who feature in the works chosen: this might lead you into other pieces by famous composers such as Mozart, Scarlatti, Beethoven, Schubert, Tchaikovsky, Gershwin and so on, or even more recent composers, such as Pamela Wedgewood, James Rae, Deirdre Cartwright, Hussein Boon and many others.

Learn to listen closely and critically; here are some suggestions:

- Try to identify instruments, keys (atonal, major, minor or modal), time signature and/or form.
- Ask yourself if the combination of instruments you hear is one you can identify (string quartet, brass band, orchestra, rock group, jazz band etc.).
- What is the texture of the piece you hear?
- Is there a particular rhythmic feature? – an ostinato? a riff? syncopation?
- Does the melody move mainly by step? by leap? through a chord? a mixture of these?
- How would you describe the accompaniment to the main melody? For example, is there an Alberti-bass pattern?

Think in terms of the Elements of Music and use them as a basis for appraising what you hear, though not always trying to cover **every** element. Try to base your listening around an easily remembered mnemonic such as **DR SMITH**.

D	Dynamics
R	Rhythm (and Metre)
S	Structure (and Form)
M	Melody
I	Instruments (Timbre)
T	Texture
H	Harmony (and Tonality)

Whenever you listen to a piece of music, focus on one or more of its musical features and listen as closely and accurately as you can. Discuss your findings with others, whether in a small group or as part of the GCSE class.

OTHER WAYS TO PREPARE FOR THE EXAMINATION

Using the 'inner ear'

Everyone can 'sing' a tune inside his or her head: this is called the 'inner ear'. You need to train your inner ear so you can 'hear' what a pattern of notes sounds like and so you can also 'hear' the notes you write down in a dictation question.

You can do this in different ways:

- Look at a short tune and try to imagine what it sounds like: think of the rhythm and the way the tune moves – up or down by step or leap. When you have had a try, play the tune over (or get somebody else to do it for you) and see how right you were. The more you practise, the better you will get.
- Imagine a short phrase in your head then try to write it down, to notate it: when you have had a try, play back what you have written (or get somebody else to do it for you) and see how close you were.
- Write a short pattern of notes onto a stave, using the treble or bass clef, depending on which you read better. Look at what you have written in terms of rhythm and pitch and try to 'hear it' in your head. When you have tried this, as before, play back what you have written (or get somebody else to do it for you) and see how close you were.

General advice

Listen to music which you have heard before and you know demonstrates the use of one or more Element of Music well; for example, you might think of the opening of the music for *Jaws* and think about its use of timbre and pitch. Imagine what this would sound like played on a glockenspiel and, therefore, at a very high pitch: it would certainly not have the same effect. Ask yourself:

- What instruments **are** used?
- What is their pitch?

Listen to dance music and try to work out the characteristic rhythms which set different dances apart from each other, whether the dance be a waltz, a polka, a minuet, a club dance, disco music and so on.

Listen to how different composers have used individual families of instruments:

- string instruments (whether in chamber groups or a string orchestra)
- brass instruments (whether orchestral brass used within an orchestra, for a fanfare, or as a brass band)
- percussion instruments, both pitched and unpitched
- woodwind instruments, whether in chamber groups of like instruments or in mixed woodwind groupings
- wind bands (i.e. using both brass and woodwind instruments), sometimes called concert wind bands or military bands
- jazz combinations, large and small; it is here that you are most likely to hear effects such as *con sordino* (with a mute) and *glissando* (slide)
- rock groups, particularly the ways guitars and percussion have been used
- vocal groups both accompanied and unaccompanied (*a cappella*).

Listen for the different effects of various instrumental techniques: *pizzicato* or plucking the strings, arco or using the bow, *col legno* or with the wood of the bow, using mutes (*con sordino*), sustaining and una corda pedals on the piano, and so on.

Listen also for the use of different types of articulation: playing smoothly (*legato*), playing in a detached manner (*staccato*), the use of ornaments (e.g. trills, mordents or turns), changing speeds (*tempi*) through *rallentando/ritardando/ritenuto* (*rall.* or *rit.*) – slowing down gradually – or *accelerando* (*accel.*) – speeding up gradually.

Above all, look in the specification at the section headed *The organisation of sound*, where each Area of Study is explained through a list of associated terms, and be sure that you understand all the musical vocabulary there. Test yourself by copying out some of the terms and then, at a later date, try to explain what they mean. Alternatively, arrange quizzes with other members of your GCSE group.

The tests in this book use excerpts from longer pieces of music: wherever possible, try to listen to more of the whole piece. A lot of the music will be new to you and can open your ears to new and exciting areas of music if you give it a chance!

In the actual examination, each excerpt will usually have two to five questions based on it and be played several times (two, three, four, even five). To help you gain most benefit from the questions in this book, each excerpt has several questions to accompany it rather than the minimum of two and some will be longer than those you are likely to find in the actual examination. Because of these factors, most excerpts should be played four times (more, if needed). Several excerpts used in this book are longer than you can expect to hear in the actual examination. This is done so that more practice can be given with a range of questions and it might be that you decide to answer just a selection from those excerpts which have rather a lot of questions attached.

CLASSROOM ACTIVITIES

RHYTHM AND METRE

Let us look at some of the most common terms we use in rhythm and metre.

1. Clap a beat (about one every second). This is a **pulse** which is **regular**.

2. Add an **accent** to every second, third or fourth clap. This creates a **metre** – either 2-, 3- or 4-time, also known as duple, triple or quadruple time.

3. Half the class clap a regular pulse in 2-, 3- or 4- time, while the other half put in two claps for every one. This will create **simple time** (a metre where every beat is divisible by 2) – either $\frac{2}{4}$, $\frac{3}{4}$, or $\frac{4}{4}$ time.

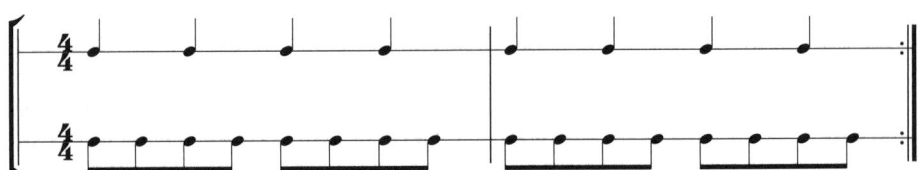

4. Half the class clap a regular pulse in 2-, 3- or 4- time, while the other half put in three claps for every one. This will create **compound time** (a metre where every beat is divisible by 3) – either $\frac{6}{8}$, $\frac{9}{8}$, or $\frac{12}{8}$ time.

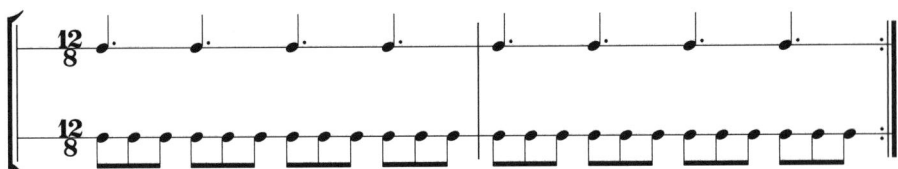

Here are a few more examples of rhythmic devices that you can try out in class.

1. Clap the following rhythm (it's the rhythm of the title of this section!).

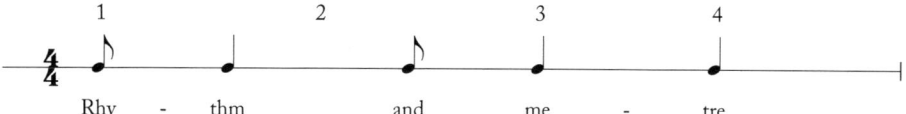

The second and third claps are between the beats (off-beat), this creates **syncopation**.

2. Now try this (you may need your teacher to help you start).

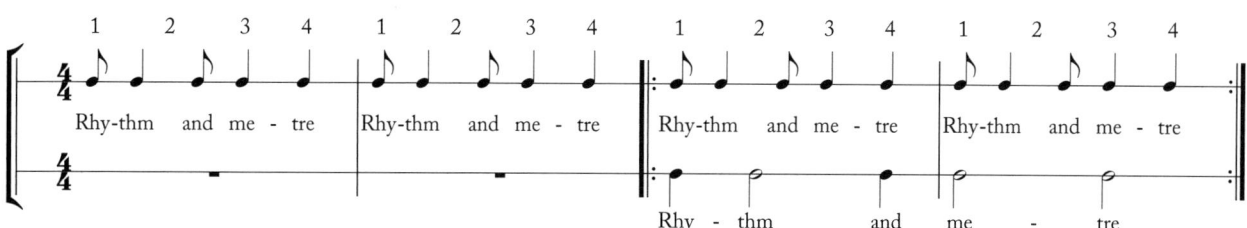

Half the class clap the rhythm of the top line and keep repeating it. Then add the other half of the class who clap the same rhythm but with each note double the value, in other words at half speed.

You have created **augmentation**.

3. Half the class clap the original rhythm (not too quickly) and keep repeating it. Then add the other half of the class who clap the same rhythm but with each note half the value, in other words at double speed.

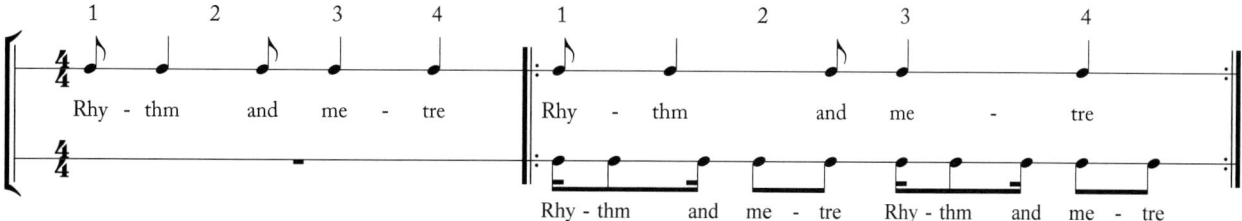

You have created **diminution**.

CLASSROOM ACTIVITIES

4. The final challenge is to try putting all three rhythms together. For the really adventurous, why not turn this into a class composition by adding melodies, different instruments/voices, dynamics etc.?

TEXTURE

We use the word **texture** to describe how musical sounds are combined. Questions on texture often ask you to use special words to describe it. Now that we are working towards GCSE we should be thinking beyond descriptions such as 'thick' or 'thin'. There are many technical terms that AQA will expect you to know and use when describing how sounds are combined. Here are the main ones, together with a brief explanation:

- **Homophonic**: sometimes known as **chordal** or **harmonic**. You should listen out for several parts moving in the same rhythm, creating a series of chords. 'The National Anthem' is a good example of this.
- **Polyphonic**: sometimes known as **contrapuntal**. This is where there are at least two lines of music which are equally important and do not move together in rhythm. There are other words which describe special types of polyphonic texture. **Canonic** describes a piece where one melody is followed in another part by the same melody: think of a round like 'London's Burning' (**Imitative** is similar to canonic – each new entry in a different part starts off the same, but then can change as it goes on.) **Layered** is a term often associated with modern recording techniques where one sound is recorded on top of another, e.g. the beginning of the Coldplay track for question 15.

18 CLASSROOM ACTIVITIES

These are the two main types of texture, but there are still a few others which need explaining:

- **Unison** and **octaves**: don't confuse these. The first is where everyone is playing or singing exactly the same notes. The second is where they are playing or singing the same pitches but at different octaves. You can easily get these wrong if you are not listening very carefully.
- **Single melody line**: this is exactly what you would expect – a solo line without accompaniment; imagine a solo bugler playing The Last Post. (This is sometimes also known as monophonic or monodic, but these terms are not really appropriate since they usually refer to music from very early periods which are not covered in this exam.)
- **Melody with accompaniment**: self-explanatory, but more able listeners will be able to describe the accompaniment in more detail. It might be a single bass line, or chords, or broken chords.
- **Antiphonal**: sometimes known as 'call-and-response'. This is where the voices or instruments are in two or more groups; they play alternately, often copying each other's music.

Take the tune 'Frère Jacques' and learn to sing it or play it in the key of C. If you can't play all of it, then the first half, which is easier, will be enough.

This is an example of **single melody line** texture.

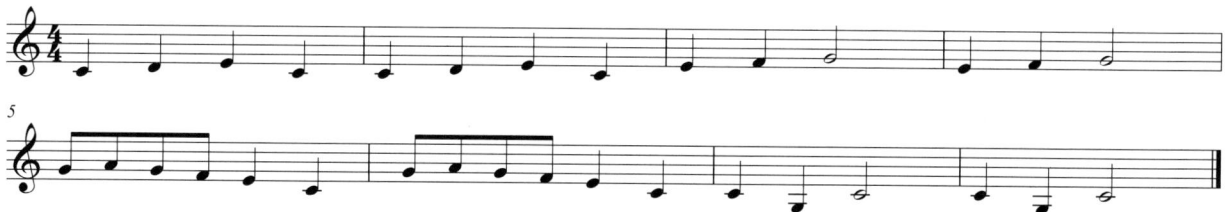

Now try all these following different methods of playing 'Frère Jacques' and decide which of the terms explained above best fits the music.

If you have access to a computer running a sequencing and/or score-writing programme such as Cubase, Garageband or Sibelius, you could try recording the different methods of playing yourself to see how different they sound. Try using different timbres for each of the different parts.

1. Play the melody with everyone starting on the same note at the same time.

CLASSROOM ACTIVITIES 19

2. Play the melody with everyone starting at the same time, but with some people starting on a higher or lower C.

3. Play the melody with people staggering their start – enter one or two bars after each other.

4. Play as in method number one, but get one person to play these chords in each bar on a keyboard instrument or guitar:

Frè	–	re	Ja – cques
C major		G major	C major (two beats)

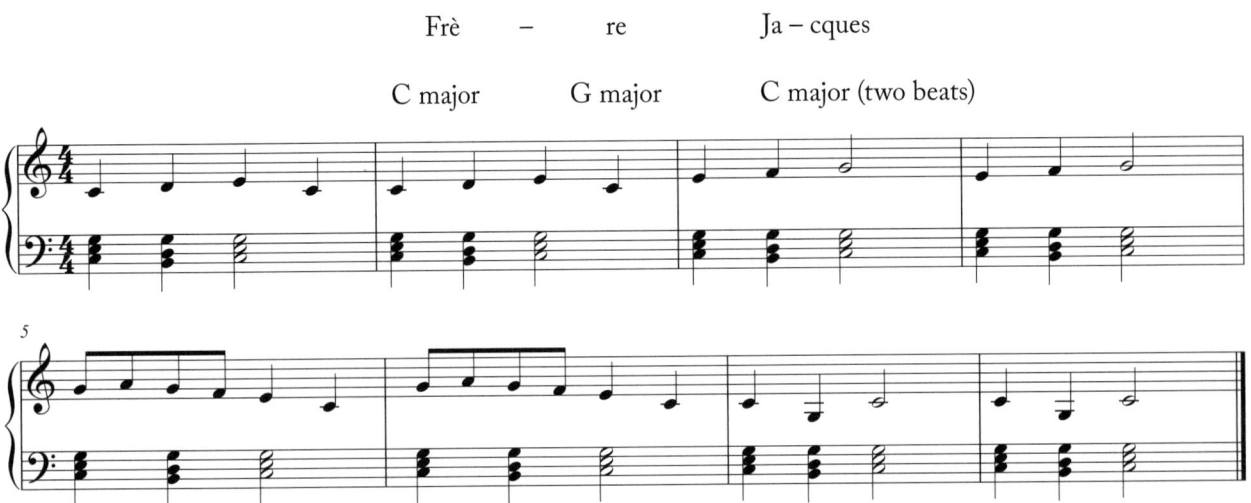

5. Half the class play all the odd numbered bars and the other half the even ones. This works well if you have a distance between the two groups.
You can have fun trying out different combinations of sounds: high/low, soft/loud, legato/staccato etc.

Did you recognise each type of texture? Here are the answers:

1. Unison
2. Octaves
3. Canon/Canonic
4. Melody with accompaniment
5. Antiphonal

For the more adventurous, you could organise a complete class performance of a much longer piece based on varieties of texture in 'Frère Jacques'. You should then have little problem in recognising the textures in the music in the Listening Test.

MELODY

It was probably Confucius who said:

- Read it – you forget it.
- See it – you remember it.
- Do it – you understand it.

Taking this maxim on board, we will tackle the terms for **melody** (as found under *The organisation of sound* in the specification) by singing or playing a round which uses many of them (and a couple more which don't come under 'melody'). When you have performed them, you will certainly remember what they sound like and have a better understanding of how they work. The terms that you need to learn are underlined in the lyrics.

When it comes to the two ornaments, we have first written them in their shorthand version and then written them out in full when they are repeated.

CLASSROOM ACTIVITIES   21

Before you perform the round, here are some brief explanations of all the terms used, as well as references to where they appear in the music – sing or play each one first before you learn the complete round:

- **ostinato** (see below): a rhythmic, harmonic or melodic pattern played many times in succession
- **triadic** (bars 13–16): a melody which uses only the notes of a triad, i.e. the root, the 3rd and the 5th
- **passing note** (bars 17–18): a decorating note which fills in the gap between two notes of a triad
- **gliss.** (bars 19–20): short for **glissando,** sliding from one note to another
- **conjunct** (bar 21): a melody in which the notes move stepwise
- **disjunct** (bar 21): a melody which leaps between notes rather than moving stepwise
- **scalic** (bar 23): a melody which follows the notes of a scale
- **acciaccatura** (bars 25–26): a decoration where the note **crushes** into the main melody note. It is played or sung as quickly as possible
- **appoggiatura** (bars 27–28): a decoration where the note **leans** into the main melody note. In this case it uses up half of the value of the main note
- **pedal** (bars 29–32): a sustained or repeated note when other parts and harmonies are changing around it. It can occur in any part, though it is most commonly found in the bass
- **broken chord** (bars 33–34): a melodic pattern where the notes of a chord are played separately
- **sequence** (bars 33–34 and 35–36): immediate repetition of a phrase in the same part but at a different pitch.

Find one person who doesn't get easily bored to sing or play the following, over and over again.

> A note on Italian pronunciation:
>
> The names for the two ornaments, 'acciaccatura' and 'appoggiatura', have been set using pronunciation as Italians would speak it, rather than in the English way that is sometimes done.
>
> acciaccatura: at–cha–ka–too–ra. The stress is on the second and fourth syllables.
>
> appoggiatura: ap–po–ja–too–ra. The stress is on the second and fourth syllables.

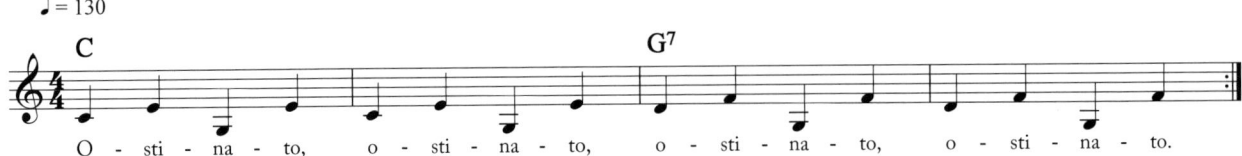

For extra support, another person could play chords on the piano or guitar.

Divide the rest of your class into, say, three groups and sing or play the following round, the second and third groups starting when the previous group has reached the point marked ⊕.

CLASSROOM ACTIVITIES

The AQA Round

THE WESTERN CLASSICAL TRADITION

QUESTION 1　　　　　　　　　　　　　　　　　　　　　0:00–0:30

This excerpt is taken from a very famous piano sonata by Mozart. As well as being a great composer, Mozart was a talented performer on both the violin and the piano. He became famous first for his playing abilities and then for his compositions.

This piano sonata is thought to have been written for one of his pupils. The excerpt is taken from the first movement but, if possible, you should try to listen to all of each movement and even play it, or parts of it!

The excerpt will be played four times. You may find it helpful to tick a box each time you hear the excerpt.

a. Which of the following outlines matches the opening melody? *Tick your answer.*

i. ☐

ii. ☐

iii. ☐

iv. ☐

(1 mark)

Hint: remember the advice given on page 10 of the Introduction of this book concerning how to approach melodic dictation: this is a different version but the advice holds good.

b. What is the time signature of this excerpt?

....

(1 mark)

Hint: check back to page 8 of the Introduction of this book and the explanation of how to work out the time signature.

c. Which of the following terms best describes the speed or tempo of this excerpt? *Circle your answer.*

      Allegro   **Largo**   **Maestoso**   **Presto**

(1 mark)

Hint: notice that these markings are for speeds/tempi which are quite different from each other. This means that there should be no reason for confusion as long as you know what each of these terms means.

d. Which of the following best describes the tonality of this excerpt? *Circle your answer.*

      atonal   **major**   **minor**   **modal**

(1 mark)

Hint: in this case – and it might well happen in the examination – you have been told who composed this music. You can, if you know when Mozart was alive, cross out some possible answers. If you aren't given the composer's name or you don't recognise it, it should soon become obvious that this excerpt is firmly in a key; in addition, it has a bright, happy feel to it and, though not always the case, this often will point you towards the right answer!

e. Describe the texture of this excerpt.

....

....

(1 mark)

5

*Hint: there is only one mark for this answer so a simple, straightforward answer will do. Two lines are given in case you want to write a few words rather than just two or three: don't think you have to fill in all the space and **don't** give the examiner a choice of answers: **you** must decide on your answer. You should think of a general way of summing up the texture of this excerpt rather than going into great detail.*

Composition activities

1. Use the first three notes of the correct answer to (a) as the basis for a short tune: add chords and write question-and-answer style phrases.

2. As a variation on this, work in a small group (three or four is good, and probably no more than six) with each member composing an opening phrase and then passing their phrase on round the group for others to add a second, third, fourth or additional phrase (depending on the size of the group). Look at how each tune has developed and discuss strengths and weaknesses.

3. Use just the opening phrase you have written – the 'Question' – and extend it through the use of a sequence, rising or falling, whichever you think sounds best.

4. Listen to the left-hand pattern in this extract and try to use this as an accompaniment to a tune you have composed or the next tune you compose.

Performing activities

- Find a short piece of music by Mozart to learn to play, either alone or with others: you might choose something from this piano sonata, from *Eine kleine Nachtmusik* or part of his variations on 'Ah! vous dirais-je, maman' (which I am sure you will recognise as a well-known nursery rhyme).
- Perform your chosen piece to members of your GCSE group and discuss how Mozart has used the different Elements in the Areas of Study.

QUESTION 2   0:00–1:00

This is the last section of Fauré's Requiem, *which is a piece of music written for a church funeral service. This music is sung when it is believed the body makes its final journey into paradise. Do you think Fauré has captured the mood well?*

The excerpt will be played four times. You may find it helpful to tick a box each time you hear the excerpt.

☐ ☐ ☐ ☐

a. Name the keyboard instrument playing.

.... *(1 mark)*

b. Which of the following best describes the melody it is playing? *Circle your answer.*

    chromatic   **conjunct**   **disjunct**   **whole-tone**

(1 mark)

c. Name the type of voices singing. Choose from the following list. *Circle your answer.*

    alto   **bass**   **tenor**   **treble**

(1 mark)

d. How many different pitches are sung in the first phrase? The words are 'In paradisum'.

.... *(1 mark)*

e. What is the time signature of this music?

.... *(1 mark)*

f. What is the tonality of this music?

.... *(1 mark)*

6

THE WESTERN CLASSICAL TRADITION   27

QUESTION 3 0:00–0:41

This excerpt is taken from Symphony No. 7 by Beethoven. It was first heard in a concert which also included his Eighth Symphony and other large-scale works: Beethoven certainly gave his paying audiences value for their money!

This excerpt will be played four times. You may find it helpful to tick a box each time you hear the excerpt.

☐ ☐ ☐ ☐

a. What is the tonality of the opening of this excerpt?

....

(1 mark)

Hint: remember the choices you have and the tips given to help you decide. If you have forgotten, look again at the Introduction of this book.

b. What is the time signature of this excerpt?

....

(1 mark)

c. Name the instruments which play the main melody.

....

(1 mark)

*Hint: start by focusing on the pitch of the instruments: you can then restrict your choice to those which can play at this pitch. From there, think in terms of the sounds of the different types of instruments – woodwind, brass, percussion, strings. Remember that few percussion instruments can play a tune and **none** did in Beethoven's time.*

d. Name the family of instruments to which they belong.

....

(1 mark)

e. Which of the following is the rhythm which features most in this excerpt? *Tick your answer.*

(1 mark)

5

Hint: work out the similarities and differences between these rhythms in advance: you will then be able to refine your choice.

Composition activities

1. Find out as much as you can about the instrument which plays the main melody – its range, characteristics, and some music written for it apart from this.

2. Find out how other composers use this instrument (and other ways in which Beethoven uses it). In particular, find out about music written to feature this instrument.

3. Using the rhythms given within (e), write a short ostinato-based composition. You can use pitched, unpitched or a combination of pitched and unpitched instruments.

Performing activities

- If there is someone in your GCSE group or in your school/college who can play the instrument identified in question (c) above, ask them to demonstrate it, showing its range, ways of playing it and various effects it can achieve.
- Perform the compositions done as a response to Composition activity 3 above.
- Ask your teacher for a copy of bars 3–18 of this movement and learn to play it on any instrument of your choice.

Extension

Work out which chords you think fit with the tune (keep it simple!) and then arrange this for a small group of players to perform.

QUESTION 4　　　　　　　　　　　　　　　　　　　　0:00–0:39

This is taken from a book of pieces by J. S. Bach which is known as 'The 48' or 'The Well-Tempered Clavier'. It was written at the point in history when major and minor scales were becoming established. Bach wrote music for each of the major and minor scales (24) and then wrote another set.

The excerpt will be played four times. You may find it helpful to tick a box each time you hear the excerpt.

☐　☐　☐　☐

a. Which of the following terms best describes the melodic movement in this excerpt? *Circle your answer.*

　　broken chords　　　**chromatic**　　　**pentatonic**　　　**scalic**

(1 mark)

b. Describe the chord heard at the very beginning of this excerpt.

　　............................

(1 mark)

c. Which of the following is the time signature of this excerpt? *Circle your answer.*

　　3/4　　　4/4　　　5/4　　　6/8

(1 mark)

d. Name the instrument playing this excerpt.

　　............................

(1 mark)

e. How does the key at the end of this excerpt relate to the key at the beginning?
Tick your answer.

i. ☐ the same key as at the beginning

ii. ☐ the relative minor

iii. ☐ the subdominant

iv. ☐ the dominant

(1 mark)

5

Hint: *if the music has gone to a minor key, your choice is simple. If it is a major key, first decide if you think it has moved from the original, the opening key. If not, your answer is (i), if it has, you must decide between (iii) and (iv). Some people can tell the difference just by the 'feel' of these keys; if you can't (and you won't be alone!), try to pitch the new key note and sing up or down to the original key note either because you can remember it or because you can remember the **new** note and then relate it to the start of the next playing of the excerpt. This is a technique you certainly will need to practise.*

Composing activities

Bach has effectively written a sequence of different chords but has made it interesting because of how they progress, how they move from one to the next.

- Try to compose a chord sequence which also has a strong sense of progression.
- Experiment with different ways of playing your chords and decide which is the most effective – and why!

Performing activities

- Try to play this piece by Bach.
- Listen to and then perform in a group his 'Air' from Orchestral Suite No. 3 in D major, BWV 1068, more popularly known as the 'Air on the G string' after an arrangement which was made of it for the violin. I am sure you will have heard this music before.

QUESTION 5   0:00–0:50 (fade)

This excerpt is taken from the second movement of Mahler's Symphony No. 1, known as the 'Titan'. Try to listen also to the third movement, based on a painting which shows animals carrying the dead body of a hunter. The main tune is based on a minor version of 'Frère Jacques'.

The excerpt will be played four times. You may find it helpful to tick a box each time you hear the excerpt.

a. The excerpt starts with just bass instruments; what is the interval between the two pitches they play? *Circle your answer.*

    major 3rd   **perfect 4th**   **perfect 5th**   **major 6th**

(1 mark)

b. Another repeating figure is added above this, notably by the 1st violins. Name the interval between the two notes they play.

....

(1 mark)

c. Fill in the missing notes in bars 11–12 below, using the rhythm provided.

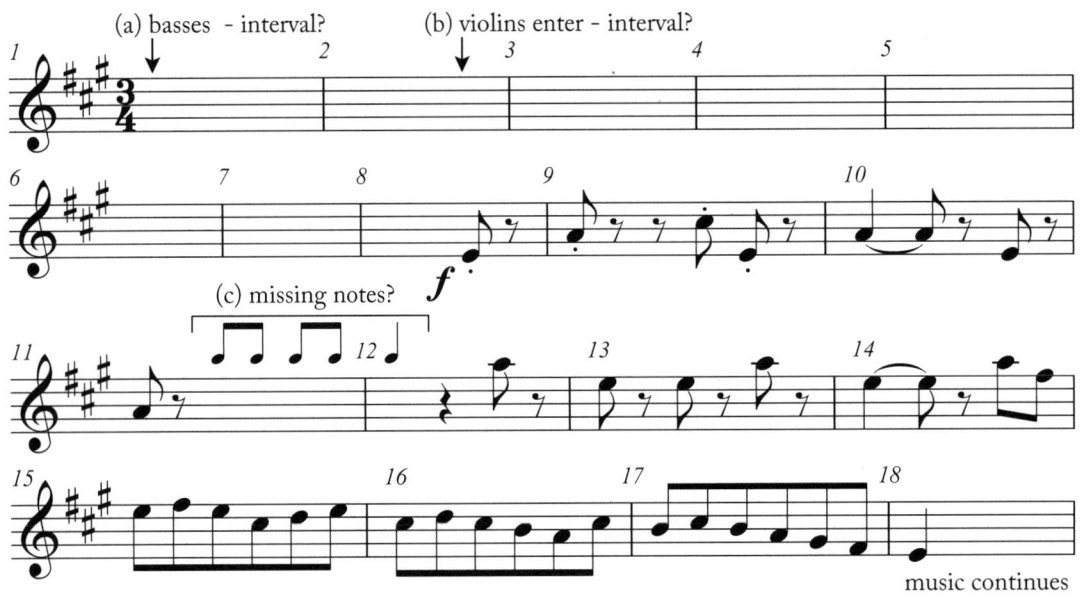

music continues

(5 marks)

7

Hint: *remember to listen carefully to the last note which is printed on the score **before** the notes you have to fill in and link this to what you hear next: is it*

- the same pitch?
- a note above?
- a note below?
- a bigger interval?

*Then listen to the note which **follows** the last one you add: does the difference in pitch sound right?*

Extension questions

Note for teachers: these can be added either to stretch the more able candidates or as additional questions for all with further playings of the excerpt.

d. Which family of instruments plays the melody from bar 8^3?

.... *(1 mark)*

e. What is the tonality of this excerpt?

.... *(1 mark)*

2

Composition activities

1. Use the bass interval as an ostinato pattern for a short composition: it can be played on any pitched instrument and you can add any instrument(s) above it.

2. This composition is a dance. Write a short dance movement in a similar style: you should aim to write two sections to make a binary-form piece.

Performing activities

- Find a short dance piece to learn.
- Perform this either as a solo or as part of a group.
- Discuss the characteristics of the dance which help create its particular style.

Further listening

As well as listening to the third movement of this symphony, listen to how other orchestral composers have used the orchestra: good examples can be found in the music of Beethoven, Bruckner, Elgar, Haydn, Mozart, Shostakovich and Tchaikovsky, to name just a few.

QUESTION 6　　　　　　　　　　　　　　　　　　0:00–0:50

This excerpt is taken from music by Mendelssohn. He is famous in many areas of music: he was a successful composer from a young age, many people have used his 'Wedding March' at the end of their marriage service, he was responsible for a new wave of interest in the music of Bach and his Violin Concerto in E minor is very popular – try to listen to it.

The excerpt will be played four times. You may find it helpful to tick a box each time you hear the excerpt.

☐ ☐ ☐ ☐

a. What is the tonality at the beginning of this excerpt? *Circle your answer.*

　　atonal　　　　major　　　　minor　　　　modal

(1 mark)

b. Which of the following ensembles is playing this excerpt? *Circle your answer.*

　　clarinet quintet　　flute quartet　　piano quintet　　string octet

(1 mark)

Hint: *think carefully about the differences between these ensembles and decide which type(s) of instruments you can hear. If there is only one family involved, the answer must be 'string octet'. If there are string instruments plus an instrument from a different family, you need to decide whether that instrument is a clarinet, a flute or a piano.*

c. What is the time signature of this excerpt?

　　.........................

(1 mark)

d. Give an Italian term to describe the tempo of this excerpt.

　　.........................

(1 mark)

Hint: *do take note that your answer must be an **Italian** term: think of the different Italian terms for tempo and **do not** use an English word.*

e. Which dynamic marking best suits this excerpt?

　　.........................

(1 mark)

f. Which of the following textures can you hear in this excerpt? *Circle **three** terms.*

antiphonal	canonic	homophonic
melody with accompaniment	single melody line	unison

(3 marks)

8

Composition activities

Try to decide what mood is created by this excerpt: is it happy, lively, sad or meditative? Discuss how the mood has been created: think in terms of tempo, texture, tonality, rhythm, harmony, melody and form.

When you have decided, try to compose a short piece of music, preferably for some of the instruments which you have heard in this excerpt (i.e. using the same timbres), which creates the same mood.

Performing activities

1. Perform any compositions written in response to the stimulus above on acoustic instruments wherever possible.

2. Try to get an arrangement of a short piece by Mendelssohn to play either as a solo or as part of a group.

Listening and Appraising activities

1. Research the instruments which make up the ensemble featured in this excerpt (i.e. the correct answer to (b)).

2. Try to listen to:

   - other music by Mendelssohn, such as his 'Wedding March', his Overture to *A Midsummer Night's Dream* (written when he was 17!) or one of his 'Songs without Words' for piano.
   - parts of the Violin Concerto in G minor by Bruch.
   - music from *Eine kleine Nachtmusik* by Mozart: this was originally written for string quartet but is more usually heard played by string orchestra.
   - the 'Dargason' from Holst's *St. Paul's Suite*: this combines a lively modal tune in $\frac{6}{8}$ with a version of 'Greensleeves'.
   - 'Playful Pizzicato' from the *Simple Symphony* by Benjamin Britten.

3. Discuss the different ways in which the composers have used string instruments and the different effects they have obtained.

THE WESTERN CLASSICAL TRADITION

QUESTION 7   0:00–1:53

Malcolm Arnold was the principal trumpeter with the London Philharmonic Orchestra and BBC Symphony Orchestra in the mid-20th century. His compositions for orchestra show that he made full use of his first-hand experience. This question concentrates on Arnold's use of instruments and illustrates what a master of orchestral writing he was.

The excerpt will be played four times. You may find it helpful to tick a box each time you hear the excerpt.

☐ ☐ ☐ ☐

a. Name the instrument which plays the descending arpeggio at the beginning.

.... (1 mark)

Hint: *there is an unintended clue in the question.*

b. Which instrument plays the first solo melody?

.... (1 mark)

c. Which of the following techniques are the violins using when they accompany this first melody? Circle **one** answer.

legato   pizzicato   staccato   tremolando

(1 mark)

d. When the strings take over the melody which of the following techniques do they use? Circle **one** answer.

con arco   con sordino   pizzicato   tremolando

(1 mark)

e. Name the instrument which takes over the melody after the strings.

.... (1 mark)

f. Which family of instruments accompanies this instrument?

.... (1 mark)

6

Composing activities

1. Write an eight-bar melody, or take one that you prepared earlier.

2. Rewrite the melody to make it suitable for different instruments. Choose instruments which are played by other members of your class. Find out which keys they like to play in (not all instruments find the key of C easy). Find out how high and low they can play, how quickly they can play, how loud they can play. Adjust your melody accordingly, changing the speed, the articulation and volume as you see fit.

Listen to it being performed and see how it has altered the mood and character of your melody.

Further listening

1. Listen to the complete movement and take note of how the melody and accompaniment continue to vary on each repetition.

2. Listen to the whole movement and notice how Arnold changes key at the start of each repetition of the melody. He moves up a major 3rd each time – very unusual, but typical of Malcolm Arnold. If you go up a major 3rd three times you arrive back in the key you started.

QUESTION 8

2:33–4:21

Tchaikovsky wrote this symphony just before he died. His death is surrounded in mystery, but some say that he committed suicide and that this music is a reflection of his severely depressed state of mind. It is certainly a heart-rending melody.

The excerpt will be played four times. You may find it helpful to tick a box each time you hear the excerpt.

☐ ☐ ☐ ☐

The first eight bars of the melody are printed below; Tchaikovsky repeats the melody three times. The first repeat has been described for you. Write your own descriptions of the next two repeats, each time showing **two** differences from the original melody and its accompaniment.

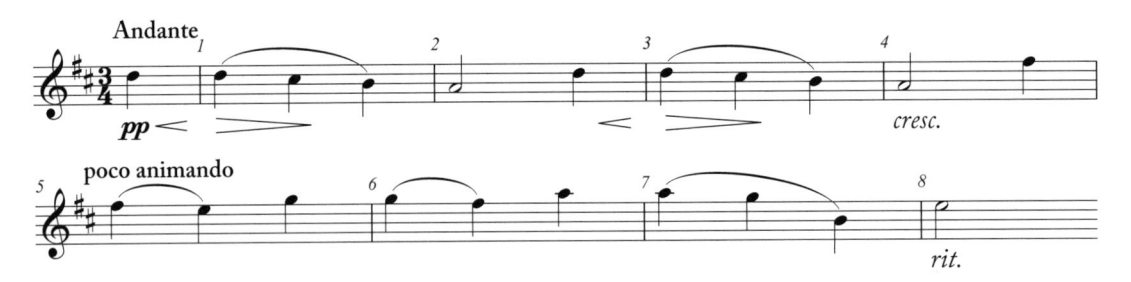

First repeat.

It is slightly louder. ✓ The trombones ✓ imitate ✓ the melody one bar later. ✓ From bar 5 ✓ the melody changes. ✓

Note: the points which gain marks have been ticked. This shows you how little you have to write to gain the marks if you are precise and clear. Try to do this in your answers.

Second repeat

....
....
....
....

(2 marks)

38 THE WESTERN CLASSICAL TRADITION

Third repeat

....

....

....

....

(2 marks)

4

*Hint: make sure you write down **musical** facts. If you can use the correct musical terms this will make your answer very clear. If you can't remember the term, write a description in your own words. It might take longer but, if it's correct, it will show that you have a good ear, and will still gain marks.*

Further listening

This excerpt of music is in a major key, but it is very sad music. Write down the musical reasons why this music is so sad. Think of the direction of the melody, the tempo, the harmonies and the way the instruments are being played.

If you listen to the whole movement, the mood is even more intense and tragic.

Composing activities

1. Write a melody in a major key but make the mood a sad one. You will have to consider tempo, rhythm, articulation, the overall pitch of the melody and the direction of the melody line.

2. Write a melody in a minor key but make the mood a happy one. Whatever you did with tempo, pitch etc. in the first one, try the opposite in this one to see if it works.

THE WESTERN CLASSICAL TRADITION

QUESTION 9 — complete track

This melody is now the national anthem of Germany, but was originally written by Haydn to celebrate the birthday of the Emperor of his country, Austria. Later he incorporated it into the string quartet which you will hear now.

The excerpt will be played four times. You may find it helpful to tick a box each time you hear the excerpt.

☐ ☐ ☐ ☐

There are **five** phrases in this melody, but it uses only **three** different four-bar tunes, **A**, **B** and **C**. Here are the first few notes of each of those tunes:

A [music notation] music continues

B [music notation] music continues

C [music notation] music continues

a. Which of the following patterns describes the form of this excerpt? *Circle your answer.*

ABBCC   ABACC   AABBC   AABCC

(1 mark)

b. Which of the three tunes ends on the tonic? *Circle your answer.*

A   B   C

(1 mark)

c. Which of the three tunes contain an acciaccatura? *Circle your answer.*

A   B   C

(1 mark)

THE WESTERN CLASSICAL TRADITION

d. Which of the three tunes contains a sforzando (*sfz*)? *Circle your answer.*

A   B   C

(1 mark)

4

Extension questions

Note for teachers: these can be added either to stretch the more able candidates or as additional questions for all with further playings of the excerpt.

e. Which of the three tunes ends with a pause (⌢)? *Circle your answer.*

A   B   C

(1 mark)

f. Which tempo marking best suits this melody? *Circle your answer.*

Allegro   Poco adagio   Rubato   Vivace

(1 mark)

2

Further listening

Listen to the rest of this movement. Haydn has written a set of variations on this melody. Write down two differences in the music of each variation.

Composing activity

Learn to play another national anthem – 'God Save the Queen' is not too difficult. Compose one variation, using at least one of the differences you spotted in Haydn's variations.

THE WESTERN CLASSICAL TRADITION   41

QUESTION 10　　　　　　　　　　　　　　　　　　　　0:00–1:19

This is the unmistakable sound of Luciano Pavarotti, the Italian tenor, singing one of his most popular songs. It is a typical song from the city of Naples in Italy, but has won international fame, trivialised in ice cream adverts and heard as the jingle on ice cream vans throughout the world.

The excerpt will be played four times. You may find it helpful to tick a box each time you hear the excerpt.

☐　☐　☐　☐

Here is a plan of this excerpt to guide you as you listen.

Introduction	Verse	Chorus
4 bars	8 bars	8 bars

Introduction

a. What is the name of the device used by the French horns in the first two bars?

．．．．．．．．．．．．．．．．．．．．．．．

(1 mark)

Verse

b. Which of the following describe the melody in the verse? *Circle **two** descriptions.*

contains blue notes　　**mainly chromatic**　　**mainly conjunct**

mainly diatonic　　**mainly disjunct**

(2 marks)

Chorus

c. Which of the following describe the melody in the chorus? *Circle **two** descriptions.*

contains acciaccaturas　　**contains appoggiaturas**

contains portamento　　**contains a sequence**　　**mainly triadic**

(2 marks)

Whole excerpt

d. The bass instruments play the same rhythm (an ostinato) in almost every bar. Which of the following is the correct rhythm? *Tick the appropriate box.*

i. ☐

ii. ☐

iii. ☐

(1 mark)

6

Further listening

Listen to the rest of the song: it is just one more verse and chorus. Notice how Pavarotti changes the music and the way he sings it. He is showing off in true Italian opera singing style, to the delight of his audience. Write down all the changes you can hear.

Composing activities

Working in pairs, one person should play the famous melody written out below. The other should experiment with different ostinato patterns as an accompaniment. It can be played with only two chords – C and G. You may use any of the rhythms given in question (d), but try some new ones too. Change the tempo and dynamics to suit the different patterns. Ask yourselves how the mood changes as you change the rhythms.

Beethoven's 'Ode to Joy'

THE WESTERN CLASSICAL TRADITION   43

QUESTION 11 0:00–0:27

This music is very popular at weddings and is often simply known as 'Here comes the bride'. Almost all the music that Wagner wrote was opera and this comes from an opera called Lohengrin. *It is more often heard without the vocal parts, though this is Wagner's original version.*

The excerpt will be played four times. You may find it helpful to tick a box each time you hear the excerpt.

☐ ☐ ☐ ☐

The excerpt starts with a short introduction.

a. Name the first instrument you hear.

.... *(1 mark)*

b. What musical term best describes what is played before the voices enter?

.... *(1 mark)*

c. What is the tonality of this excerpt?

.... *(1 mark)*

d. What is the time signature of this excerpt?

.... *(1 mark)*

e. What term best describes the vocal texture of this excerpt?

.... *(1 mark)*

f. What type of choir is singing this excerpt? *Circle your answer.*

    barbershop choir   boys' choir   male-voice choir   mixed-voice choir

(1 mark)

6

Composition activities

Using the theme of a wedding, compose some music to be played as the bride walks down the aisle at the beginning of the service. Think carefully about the mood you need to create and how to use the Elements of Music to help you achieve this.

Performing activities

Get the music of the 'Bridal March' and arrange it for different groups of players within your GCSE class. Rehearse and perform it to the rest of the class.

Listening and Appraising activity

This music is most often heard played on the church organ (or pipe organ, as it is also known). Try to get hold of a recording of this version and compare the effect with Wagner's original.

QUESTION 12　　　　　　　　　　　　　　　　　　　　0:00–0:24

This is part of a much longer piece by Mozart. It was very fashionable in Mozart's time to write music in the style of music from exotic countries like Turkey. The last movement of this piece is called 'Rondo Alla Turca'. Try to listen to it and see if you can spot the Turkish sounds that he has added to his music.

The excerpt will be played four times. You may find it helpful to tick a box each time you hear the excerpt.

☐　☐　☐　☐

a. What is the time signature of this music?

....

(1 mark)

b. This music has two phrases. Name or describe the cadence at the end of each phrase.

i. First phrase ....

ii. Second phrase ....

(4 marks)

c. Which of the following rhythmic features can you hear? *Circle your answer.*

augmentation　　　cross-rhythm　　　dotted rhythm　　　polyrhythm

(1 mark)

6

Composing activities

1. Write a melody using only the first five notes of the major or minor scale. It should last four bars and sound unfinished.

2. Write a second phrase which is almost the same as the first, but change the ending to make it sound finished.

3. Add a second part which has the same rhythm as the first, but it should always be a 3rd away from the first. You will have to decide whether it sounds best to be a 3rd above or below. Sometimes you may have to switch in mid-phrase.

Performing activities

1. Play your two-part melody with different instrumental or vocal combinations.

2. You may have to transpose the notes for certain instruments. Ask your teacher how to do this.

3. Discuss which combinations sound the best.

QUESTION 13   0:00–0:50

'In his youth, and well into his old age, he played the violin with a clear, penetrating tone.' This is what Johann Sebastian Bach's son, Carl Philip Emmanuel, said of his father. J.S. Bach would often lead performances of his own pieces while playing the harpsichord or the violin. (Conductors did not become the fashion until much later.)

The excerpt will be played four times. You may find it helpful to tick a box each time you hear the excerpt.

☐ ☐ ☐ ☐

a. What is the tonality of this music? *Circle your answer.*

        atonal   **major**   **minor**   **modal**

(1 mark)

b. Which time signature best fits this music? *Circle your answer.*

        $\frac{12}{8}$ $\frac{9}{8}$ $\frac{4}{4}$ $\frac{2}{4}$

(1 mark)

c. When the second violin enters, write down one similarity and one difference between the melodies of the two violins.

    i. Similarity

    ....

    ....

    ii. Difference

    ....

    ....

(2 marks)

d. Name the keyboard instrument which is accompanying.

    ....

(1 mark)

5

Composing activities

1. Work out the first four notes of this melody (listen to it a few more times if necessary). Continue it to make a melody which is eight bars long.

2. Now add another line which imitates the first for a few notes. Try starting the second line a little higher.

3. Choose instruments which suit the melodies you have written. It would make sense to write for instruments that you and your friends can play. Then you can try them out. Ask the players if the music was well written for the instruments.

Further listening

Listen to some more music by Bach. If you like very high trumpet playing then try the first movement of his Brandenburg Concerto No. 2. If it's really fast keyboard playing you are looking for, then Brandenburg Concerto No. 5 is for you. For a really relaxing melody, listen to the Air from his Orchestral Suite No. 3, known as the 'Air on the G String.'

POPULAR MUSIC OF THE 20TH AND 21ST CENTURIES

QUESTION 14   0:00–1:11

This song has often been used as background music for films, adverts and even BBC news programmes.

The excerpt will be played four times. You may find it helpful to tick a box each time you hear the excerpt.

☐ ☐ ☐ ☐

a. Name the keyboard instrument which plays at the very start.

....

(1 mark)

b. In the introduction, the metre changes every fourth bar. On the stave below, write in the time signature of the fourth bar. The time signature of the first three bars has been given to you.

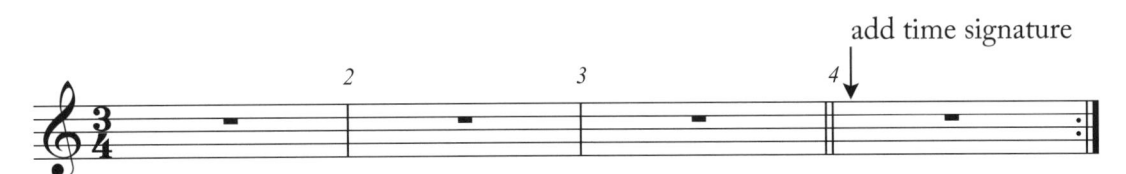

(1 mark)

Hint: *these four bars play over and over again. But if you don't get the answer, listen to what happens at the end of the excerpt.*

c. The singer's opening melody is written out below. Complete the melody on the words 'Throughout the' in bar 9, using the given rhythm.

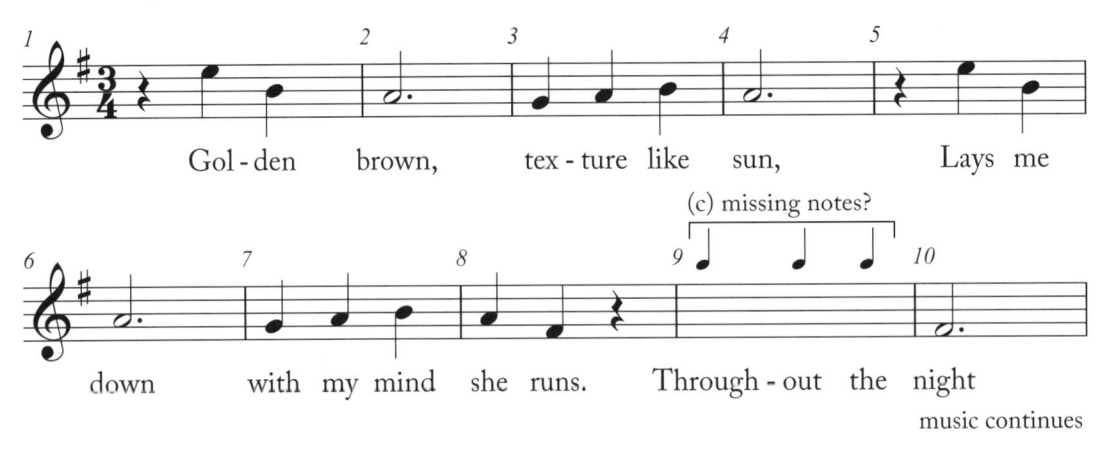

Gol-den brown, tex-ture like sun, Lays me down with my mind she runs. Through-out the night

music continues

(3 marks)

50 POPULAR MUSIC OF THE 20TH AND 21ST CENTURIES

Hint: listen carefully to the notes just before and just after the ones you have to write. Make sure your notes make musical sense.

d. Which of the following best describes the texture of the singing? *Circle your answer.*

antiphonal   contrapuntal

imitative   melody with accompaniment

(1 mark)

6

Composing activities

1. Play a few bars of 'um–cha' C-major chords, i.e. a bass note followed by a chord.

2. Change it to 'um–cha–cha', making a triple time metre.

3. Experiment with quickly changing metres, by adding or taking away chords.

4. When you find a combination of metres that you like, repeat it in four-bar phrases, using two bars of tonic (C) and two bars of dominant (G major) chords.

5. Add a melody on the top.

Further Listening and Performing activity

1. Listen to the whole of the track of 'Golden Brown' and particularly to the sections later on where first the guitar improvises over the opening four-bar phrase and then the voice improvises in a similar way.

2. Take your four-bar phrase and improvise vocally over it, using nonsense syllables (scat singing). You might imitate the sound of an electric guitar or any other instrument you wish.

QUESTION 15　　　　　　　　　　　　　　　　　　0:00–1:13

This album was produced only a week after the events of 11 September 2001 in the United States of America. The lyrics of this song are strange and puzzling, but the very first line is surely not a coincidence.

The excerpt will be played four times. You may find it helpful to tick a box each time you hear the excerpt.

☐ ☐ ☐ ☐

a. Each bar of the intro has the same piano melody. What is the name for this musical device?

.... *(1 mark)*

b. This melody has eight quavers. Mark the accents by placing an accent > over **three** of the notes on the stave below.

(3 marks)

Hint: this is also the drum rhythm when it comes in later. The snare drum is struck on each of the accents.

c. How many different chords are used in this excerpt?

.... *(1 mark)*

d. Write down one similarity and one difference between the first two lines of this song. The words are:

'The lights go out and I can't be saved.
Tides that I tried to swim against.'

Similarity

....

....

POPULAR MUSIC OF THE 20TH AND 21ST CENTURIES

Difference

....

....

(2 marks)

7

Composition activities

1. Take a bar of eight quavers and put three accents in different places until you find a rhythm that you like.

2. Create a melodic pattern with this rhythm, using the notes of a triad adding a 7th if you wish (ask your teacher about this if you're not sure).

3. Move this pattern up or down in each bar to create a four-bar phrase. Repeat this four-bar phrase as the basis for your own Coldplay-style piece.

4. Add a bass line, which could be as simple as one note per bar.

5. Add a melody using longer notes.

Further listening activities

Listen to the whole track of 'Clocks' and notice how Coldplay have put together a song of over five minutes with very little musical material.

1. One musical idea goes through the whole song. What is it?

2. How many minutes go by before the chord pattern mentioned in question (c) changes?

3. Write down a plan of the whole song. You may use whatever method you like: letters such as **ABAB**, or words like intro, verse, chorus, outro etc. Listen to it as many times as you wish, adding more and more detail to your plan, such as when instruments/voices come in and out.

QUESTION 16

0:00–0:49

Basing the lyrics of a song on topical events of the day is not new. Gilbert and Sullivan wrote songs in the 19th century about wealthy businessmen like W.H. Smith. Can you think of recent songs which have drawn attention to so-called 'fat cats'?

The excerpt will be played four times. You may find it helpful to tick a box each time you hear the excerpt.

☐ ☐ ☐ ☐

a. This is in $\frac{4}{4}$ time. How many bars are there in the introduction? *Circle your answer.*

    2   3   4   5

(1 mark)

b. What is the value of the notes played by the hi-hat cymbal in the introduction? *Circle your answer.*

    crotchet   minim   quaver   semiquaver

(1 mark)

c. The song starts with the words:

'Do the Wall Street Shuffle.
Hear the money rustle.'

Describe one difference between the way these two lines are sung.

....

(1 mark)

d. There is a new section which begins with the words 'You need a yen'. Describe what the bass guitar plays in this section.

....

....

(2 marks)

Hint: *note how many marks are allocated. This should tell you how much detail is needed.*

POPULAR MUSIC OF THE 20TH AND 21ST CENTURIES

e. Give the names of the types of voices used in the last two lines: 'You gotta be cool on Wall Street'. *Choose two from the list below.*

        alto   bass   falsetto   soprano   tenor

i. 1st line ....

ii. 2nd line ....

(2 marks)

7

Teacher advice: you may wish to trim this question down to suit your students. Alternatively, keep the question as it stands but give extra playings for those who need it.

Further listening

Listen to this track with headphones. How can you tell that this is a studio recording? Write down all the studio effects that you can hear. How different would this sound if it were performed live? You can find a live performance on YouTube to compare.

Composing/Performing activity

1. Work out the melody of the riff 'Do the Wall Street Shuffle'.

2. Play it four times, but make a slight change to it each time so that it builds in tension each time. You may add another part on the top, add a bass line, get louder, get quicker, slightly change the melody or the rhythm.

3. Listen again to the original version to compare results.

QUESTION 17   0:00–1:04

This song comes from the musical Oklahoma! *by Richard Rodgers and Oscar Hammerstein II. The musical contains several stories which unfold alongside each other and this song deals with the long-standing feud and lack of trust between farmers and cowmen (or ranchers): i.e. those who plant crops and, therefore, build fences and those who have large herds of cattle and, as a result, want the land to remain unfenced.*

The excerpt will be played four times. You may find it helpful to tick a box each time you hear the excerpt.

☐ ☐ ☐ ☐

a. Name the woodwind instrument which plays a 'fill' after each of the first two phrases.

....   *(1 mark)*

b. What is the time signature of this excerpt?

....   *(1 mark)*

c. What is the tonality of this excerpt?

....   *(1 mark)*

These are the lyrics to the first verse sung by a solo voice:

'The farmer and the cowman should be friends;
Oh, the farmer and the cowman should be friends;
One man likes to push a plough, the other likes to chase a cow,
But that's no reason why they can't be friends.'

d. When the solo voice enters, which instrument plays the 'fill' after the first two phrases?

....   *(1 mark)*

POPULAR MUSIC OF THE 20TH AND 21ST CENTURIES

e. Describe the instrumental melodic movement between 'But that's no reason why they can't be friends' and the following 'Territory folks should stick together'.

....

....

(2 marks)

6

Teaching point: note that there are two marks available here. The answer must, therefore, describe two different things about the melodic movement. Responses should address both the nature of the melodic movement – e.g. scalic, stepwise, conjunct, triadic, disjunct etc. – and its direction – e.g. rising, falling, rising and falling etc.

Extension questions

Note for teachers: these can be added either to stretch the more able candidates or as additional questions for all with further playings of the excerpt.

f. Referring to the lyrics of the first verse, name the cadences at the end of lines two and four.

  i. Line 2: ....

  ii. Line 4: ....

(2 marks)

g. In line 3, the lyrics 'One man likes to' and 'the other likes to' are sung to the chord of C major/tonic/I. Name the chord used for the words 'push a plough' and 'chase a cow'.

.... *(1 mark)*

3

POPULAR MUSIC OF THE 20TH AND 21ST CENTURIES 57

QUESTION 18 0:00–0:40

This group was originally the backing group for Cliff Richard before also making a career for themselves with their distinctive style. Originally known as The Drifters, they changed their name to The Shadows to avoid confusion with a famous American group. Many teenagers bought guitars and tried to imitate them.

The excerpt will be played four times. You may find it helpful to tick a box each time you hear the excerpt.

☐ ☐ ☐ ☐

a. Describe the rhythm played at the very beginning of this excerpt.

....

....

(2 marks)

b. Name the instrument which plays the opening riff.

....

(1 mark)

c. Name one playing technique you can hear in this part.

....

(1 mark)

d. The opening riff is played twice. Which of the following patterns best fits the form of the melody which follows? *Circle your answer.*

AAAB   AABB   AABA   ABAB   ABCA

(1 mark)

e. How many players are involved in this performance?

....

(1 mark)

6

POPULAR MUSIC OF THE 20TH AND 21ST CENTURIES

Composition activity

Using the opening rhythm, add a two-bar riff and use this as the basis for a short composition where the melody follows the same pattern as the answer to question (d).

Performing activity

Listen to a guitar player demonstrating the different techniques that can be used, including pitch bend, hammer-on, power chords, glissando, finger-picking, strumming chords, the use of distortion and other effects, and so on.

QUESTION 19   0:00–1:21

Billy Elliot tells the story of a boy from working-class roots in the north-east of England who fought against prejudice to become a professional dancer. Not only was it difficult for a boy to dance as a profession, but his desire to become a classical ballet dancer was unheard of. This track is the finale of the musical when Billy is living his dream.

The excerpt will be played four times. You may find it helpful to tick a box each time you hear the excerpt.

☐ ☐ ☐ ☐

First section (begins with feet tapping)

a. Mark with a cross (**X**) where the saxophones play at the beginning. The first has been given to you. *Add **three** more.*

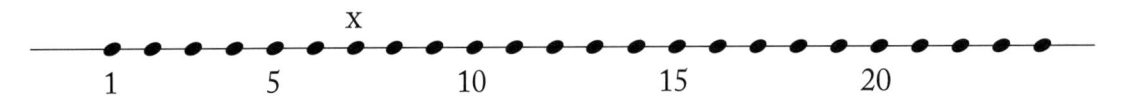

```
            X
——•—•—•—•—•—•—•—•—•—•—•—•—•—•—•—•—•—•—•—•—•—•—•——
  1       5         10        15        20
```

(3 marks)

b. What is the Italian term which describes the tempo change in this section?

....

(1 mark)

c. What is the time signature of this section?

....

(1 mark)

Second section (after the short silence)

d. What is the name of the technique used by the drummer at the start of this section?

....

(1 mark)

e. What kind of instrumental group is playing in this section? *Circle your answer.*

    big band   brass band   saxophone quartet   symphony orchestra

(1 mark)

Further listening

Listen to the rest of this track and try to identify examples of all of the following; tick the box only when you are sure you have heard it.

- ☐ Pedal note
- ☐ Rallentando
- ☐ Walking bass
- ☐ A section where the metre swings between $\frac{3}{4}$ and $\frac{6}{8}$
- ☐ Swung quavers
- ☐ Straight quavers
- ☐ The key changes up by one semitone
- ☐ Trombone glissando

You can do this individually or as a group.

QUESTION 20

version A: 0:00–0:35

version B: 0:00–0:58

These two excerpts feature different versions of the same song: the first was a No. 1 hit in 1961 for Elvis Presley, still thought of by many as simply 'The King', while the second was a cover version from 1993 by UB40, released on their Promises and Lies *album.*

Each excerpt will be played three times. You may find it helpful to tick a box each time you hear the excerpt.

A ☐   B ☐   A ☐   B ☐   A ☐   B ☐

Compare these two versions in terms of **rhythm**, **metre**, **texture**, **melody**, **timbre** and **structure**. You should aim to make a comment on each element.

....
....
....
....
....
....
....
....
....

(8 marks)

8

Teaching point

As there is no need to present the answer as continuous prose, encourage pupils to adopt a 'bullet point' approach. The most important thing is to be clear which of the two versions is being commented upon at all times. As there are eight marks available, pupils should feel free to make additional points: they will gain credit in this sort of question for each valid comment made (there is no penalty for making a comment which does not appear in the Mark Scheme).

As an alternative approach, you might like to make this sort of question 'competitive' and let your pupils work either alone or in small groups to see who can make the most valid comments.

QUESTION 21   0:00–0:34

This was a big hit for Blondie, an American pop/rock band founded by Debbie Harry and Chris Stein. Their first European success was 'Denis', which reached the charts in March 1978. The song featured here, 'Heart of Glass', was a million-seller later that same year.

The excerpt will be played four times. You may find it helpful to tick a box each time you hear the excerpt.

☐   ☐   ☐   ☐

a. What is the time signature of this excerpt?

....   *(1 mark)*

b. How many bars are played **before** the entry of the guitars?

....   *(1 mark)*

Teaching point: in this question, the answer to (a) will have a direct bearing on what will be accepted as a correct response.

c. Name the family of instruments featured in these bars.

....   *(1 mark)*

d. What is heard just before the entry of the drum kit? *Circle your choice.*

      accelerando   **acciaccatura**   **glissando**   **rubato**

                                                                                                                                                         (1 mark)

e. Which of the following is heard in the guitar part? *Circle your choice.*

      echo   **hammer-on**   **pitch bend**   **power chord**

                                                                                                                                                         (1 mark)

5

POPULAR MUSIC OF THE 20TH AND 21ST CENTURIES

QUESTION 22　　　　　　　　　　　　　　　　　　　0:00–1:08

This beautiful song comes from the musical Les Misérables *by Alain Boublil and Claude-Michel Schönberg. It is sung by Cosette. Try to listen to all of this song and, if at all possible, see the musical.*

The excerpt will be played four times. You may find it helpful to tick a box each time you hear the excerpt.

☐　☐　☐　☐

a. Which of the following musical devices can be heard under the first two phrases of the introduction to this excerpt? *Circle your choice.*

　　drum fill　　　　**ground bass**　　　　**pedal**　　　　**riff**

(1 mark)

Teaching point: *make sure that each of these terms is fully understood in advance of tackling this question. Where uncertainty exists, play examples to illustrate each of them.*

b. Which of the following pitch outlines matches the notes sung to the first line of the lyrics:

'There is a castle on a cloud,'

It is repeated on the first line of verse 2:

'There is a room that's full of toys.'

Tick your choice.

i. ☐

ii. ☐

iii. ☐

iv. ☐

(1 mark)

POPULAR MUSIC OF THE 20TH AND 21ST CENTURIES

c. What is the tonality of this excerpt?

.... *(1 mark)*

d. Name or describe the cadence in verse 1 on the words 'me to sweep.'

Verse 1

'There is a castle on a cloud,
I like to go there in my sleep,
Aren't any floors for me to sweep,
Not in my castle on a cloud.'

It is repeated in verse 2 on the words 'talks too loud':

'There is a room that's full of toys,
There are a hundred boys and girls,
Nobody shouts or talks too loud,
Not in my castle on a cloud.'

....

....

(2 marks)

e. Which of the following patterns best fits the structure of the melody of each of these verses? *Circle your choice.*

    AAAB $A^1A^2A^1B$ $A^1A^2B^1B^2$ A^1A^2BC

(1 mark)

6

Composing activity

Using the musical device which is the correct answer to (a), compose a short piece of music based on this using any instruments of your choice.

QUESTION 23 0:00–1:35 (fade)

John Williams wrote the music for the film Schindler's List, *a film about the rescue of Jewish refugees during the Second World War. He asked Itzhak Perlman to play the violin solo on the soundtrack, a poignant choice as Perlman was born in Israel just as that war was ending.*

The excerpt will be played four times. You may find it helpful to tick a box each time you hear the excerpt.

☐ ☐ ☐ ☐

a. Name the instrument playing the melody in the introduction.

....

(1 mark)

After the introduction the violin plays the following melody.

(b) missing notes?
(c) cadence?
(d) cadence?

music continues

5

b. Add the missing notes in bar 4.

(3 marks)

POPULAR MUSIC OF THE 20TH AND 21ST CENTURIES

c. Name or describe the cadence at bar 8.

....

(2 marks)

d. Name or describe the cadence at bar 10.

....

(2 marks)

e. When the violin repeats this melody, how is it different?

....

(1 mark)

9

Composing activity

At a keyboard, work out some suitable chords which will fit this melody. To get you started, the first full bar will work with a G minor chord throughout. Try to use as few chords as possible, just one or two chords per bar. If you are not a keyboard player, ask someone to record the melody into an electronic keyboard so that you can concentrate on the chords. Single finger chord facilities on the keyboard make it even easier, but avoid using it with a rhythm.

If you got the cadences right in the listening test, you should be able to find those chords quickly.

Performing activity

When everyone has finished this composing activity, play each other's work as duets and discuss the different effects of the harmonisations you have created.

POPULAR MUSIC OF THE 20TH AND 21ST CENTURIES

QUESTION 24

version A: 0:00–0:55
version B: 0:00–1:22

This is probably the most famous anti-war song of the 20th century, sung here by two of the most popular singers of that century. It was recently used in an advertising campaign highlighting the environmental-friendliness of a British supermarket chain, showing the power of popular music in the retail business.

You will hear two versions of the song 'Blowin' in the Wind', in the following order:

Version A   Version B   Version A   Version B   Version B

You may find it helpful to tick the boxes each time you hear an excerpt.

A ☐   B ☐   A ☐   B ☐   B ☐

Listen to the two versions of this song and write down differences between them. A description of the version by Bob Dylan is below. Comment on **timbre, rhythm and metre,** and **melody.**

Bob Dylan's version

The accompaniment is just an acoustic guitar and the melody is sung by Dylan alone. He adds a harmonica melody after the chorus. The melody is sung with little decoration and is all at one dynamic level. The accompaniment is a simple guitar strum throughout. The tempo is a constant, fairly brisk pace.

Stevie Wonder's version

....
....
....
....
....
....
....

(8 marks)

8

POPULAR MUSIC OF THE 20TH AND 21ST CENTURIES

Further listening

1. There are countless versions of this song. Track down as many as possible and do the same exercise as above.

2. There is now nothing to stop you doing exactly the same with covers of any songs you come across. Share your answers with others in your class and ask your teacher to check your answers.

QUESTION 25   0:00–0:42

ABBA was a very famous group whose first major hit, 'Waterloo', was performed at the Eurovision Song Contest in 1974, the first time Sweden had ever won this competition. Following that, they went on to record many other hit records, including the song featured in this question (though this version is by The ABBA Tribute Band).

The excerpt will be played four times. You may find it helpful to tick a box each time you hear the excerpt.

☐ ☐ ☐ ☐

Comment on the introduction and the setting of the following words in terms of **rhythm, texture, melody** and/or **timbre**.

> 'I'm nothing special, in fact I'm a bit of a bore;
> If I tell a joke, you've probably heard it before;
> But I have a talent, a wonderful thing,
> 'cause everyone listens when I start to sing.
> 5 I'm so grateful and proud
> All I want is to sing it out loud.'

....
....
....
....
....
....
....
....

(8 marks)

8

Teaching point*: there are, in fact, more than eight points which can be drawn from this passage and you might like to set this as (i) a group activity, where the members combine to think of as many answers as possible, or (ii) as a sort of competition with a small prize for the person who thinks of the most valid points, or (iii) as a 'stretch' exercise for the more able.*

WORLD MUSIC

QUESTION 26   0:00–0:58

Salif Keita has made his way as a musician in spite of many personal difficulties. In his native country he was an outcast because of his albinism. He also finally decided to leave to escape the political unrest in his country. He moved to Paris, but he retains a lot of the musical roots of his homeland.

The excerpt will be played four times. You may find it helpful to tick a box each time you hear the excerpt.

☐ ☐ ☐ ☐

a. What is the Italian term which describes the dynamic change at the beginning?

....   *(1 mark)*

b. Name **two** of the percussion instruments that are playing.

....

....   *(2 marks)*

c. There are **five** main phrases in the melody. Which of the following best describes the plan of the melody? *Circle your answer.*

      A^{1}A^{2}A^{1}BA^1 A^{1}BBA^{1}A^2 A^{1}A^{2}A^{1}BB   A^{1}A^{2}BBB

(1 mark)

d. Which term best describes the vocal range of the singer? *Circle your answer.*

    bass   soprano   tenor   treble

(1 mark)

5

QUESTION 27
0:00–0:32

This excerpt features a range of instruments including some from Africa. It has almost a hypnotic effect.

The excerpt will be played five times. You may find it helpful to tick a box each time you hear the excerpt.

☐ ☐ ☐ ☐ ☐

a. Which of the following scales is used in this extract? *Circle your choice.*

        major   minor   modal   pentatonic

(1 mark)

Hint: it would be a good idea to revise these scales if you are unsure about the differences between them.

b. Which pitched percussion instrument is playing this opening section?

....

(1 mark)

Teaching point: this type of question might follow a lesson on pitched and unpitched percussion.

c. Which of the following matches the recurring rhythm in the bass drum? *Tick your choice.*

i. ☐

ii. ☐

iii. ☐

iv. ☐

(1 mark)

Hint: remember to work out the different rhythms in your head before the excerpt is played. You will have to listen carefully for the bass drum pattern.

WORLD MUSIC

d. Each phrase played by tuned percussion instruments starts with the same pattern: how is the melody continued to introduce variety?

....

....

(2 marks)

e. Describe what the string instruments add after several repetitions of the opening idea.

....

....

(2 marks)

7

Composition activity

Use the type of scale which is the correct answer to question (a) as the basis for a short composition. You can choose any instruments you wish for your piece but, if available, try to use the tuned percussion instrument – or something similar – as featured in this excerpt.

Performing activities

1. Work with others to perform your composition.

2. Using a given opening phrase, improvise different ways of extending it using a 'call and response' structure: one member of the group plays the main phrase, other members take it in turns to answer it or 'respond.'

WORLD MUSIC

QUESTION 28　　　　　　　　　　　　　　　　0:00–0:42 (fade)

Here is some lively music which always seems to create a happy atmosphere. The main instruments were made from what would otherwise have been a waste product – and what a great sound they make.

The excerpt will be played four times. You may find it helpful to tick a box each time you hear the excerpt.

☐ ☐ ☐ ☐

a. Name the tuned percussion instruments playing in this excerpt.

   .... *(1 mark)*

b. Name the rhythmic device heard in the melody.

   .... *(1 mark)*

c. What is the time signature of this excerpt?

   .... *(1 mark)*

d. Comment on the second section where the melody instruments stop playing in terms of its use of **rhythm** and **texture**.

   ....

   ....

   ....

   (3 marks)

6

Hint: *think of the various terms you know from your work on Area of Study 1 and then use those which seem most appropriate. There are 3 marks and so you need to try to find three different things to say. Concentrate your answer on the two Elements of Music named.*

Composition activities

1. Research the instruments identified as the answer to (a) and learn as much as you can about their characteristics and the music written for them.

2. Using the rhythmic device identified as the answer to (b), write a short piece of music which makes use of this feature.

WORLD MUSIC

Performing activities

1. Work with others to perform your composition.

2. In a group, decide on three or four different rhythms. Play them on different percussion instruments, some pitched, some unpitched. Vary the number of instruments playing at any one time and also think in terms of form and dynamics. Try to record your performance so that you can listen to it and fully appreciate the different effects achieved.

QUESTION 29　　　　　　　　　　　　　　　　　　　　　0:00–0:39

This song is the title track of Max Romeo's album *War Ina Babylon* and describes the violent mood between the various factions in the 1972 general election in Jamaica.

The excerpt will be played four times. You may find it helpful to tick a box each time you hear the excerpt.

☐　☐　☐　☐

a. Describe the texture of the singers' music.

.... *(1 mark)*

b. Which of the following is the rhythm of the words 'War Ina Babylon'?
Tick the appropriate box.

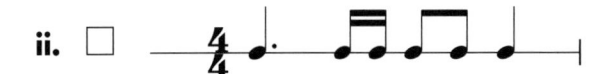

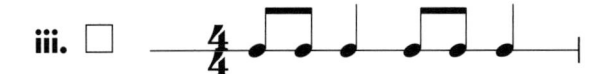

i. ☐

ii. ☐

iii. ☐

iv. ☐

(1 mark)

c. Which instrument plays the tune with the singers on the words 'War Ina Babylon'?

.... *(1 mark)*

d. On which beats of the bar does the rhythm guitar play?

.... *(2 mark)*

Hint: note how many marks are allocated. This should give you a clue about your answer.

WORLD MUSIC

e. What is the note value of the tambourine's rhythm? *Circle one of the following.*

      crotchet   **minim**   **quaver**   **semiquaver**

(1 mark)

Further listening

Amazingly, this song, which is almost five minutes long, uses only two chords throughout. Which two chords are used? How is our interest maintained in what you would expect to be a very dull, monotonous song?

Think carefully about simply doing a straight repeat in any of your compositions. Sometimes it may be perfectly acceptable, but it can also be very boring. Take ideas from your listening experiences like this one and try to make use of them in your own writing.

QUESTION 30   0:00–0:46

This is an excerpt taken from a style of music which had a great influence on some very famous pop musicians in the 1960s, inspiring some to learn the instrument and to use it in their pop songs.

The excerpt will be played four times. You may find it helpful to tick a box each time you hear the excerpt.

☐ ☐ ☐ ☐

a. Name the instrument playing this excerpt.

....

(1 mark)

b. Which of the following can you hear? *Circle your answer.*

    distortion   **glissando**   **pitch bend**   **tremolo**

(1 mark)

c. Which harmonic term best describes the accompaniment to the main melody?

....

(1 mark)

d. Comment on this excerpt in terms of its use of rhythm and metre.

....

....

....

(3 marks)

6

Hint: think of the various terms you know from your work on Area of Study 1 and then use those which seem most appropriate. There are 3 marks and so you need to try to find three different things to say.

78   WORLD MUSIC

Composition activities

1. Research the instrument identified as the answer to (a) and learn as much as you can about its characteristics and the music written for it, both traditional and how it was used in pop music.

2. Using the harmonic device identified as the answer to (c), write a short piece of music making use of this feature.

Performing activities

1. Work with others to perform your composition.

2. In a group, decide on one or two notes to be played as a drone and then take it in turns to improvise over it, basing your improvisation on a particular rhythm, a small group of notes, a pentatonic scale, and so on. Keep the drone going, but pass it between the members of the group to be played on different instruments at different pitches. Try to record your performance so that you can listen to it and fully appreciate the different effects achieved.

QUESTION 31 0:00–0:42

This excerpt is a good example of fusion music: much modern music combines styles and characteristics from different parts of the world. Which two styles are combined here?

Hint: The linking factor is Jamaica and the Caribbean.

The excerpt will be played four times. You may find it helpful to tick a box each time you hear the excerpt.

☐ ☐ ☐ ☐

a. What is the tonality of this excerpt?

.... *(1 mark)*

b. What is the time signature of this excerpt?

.... *(1 mark)*

c. The opening melody is accompanied by four different chords. How often does the accompanying chord change?

.... *(1 mark)*

d. Which of the following statements is correct in terms of the four chords used in this excerpt? *Tick your choice.*

i. ☐ They rise by step.

ii. ☐ They fall by step.

iii. ☐ They are I/tonic – VI/submediant – IV/subdominant – V/dominant.

iv. ☐ They are I/tonic – V/dominant – II/supertonic – IV/subdominant.

(1 mark)

4

WORLD MUSIC

Composition activities

1. Use the chord sequence which is the correct answer to (d) as the basis for a short composition. You can choose any instruments you wish but might find it useful to play the chords on a keyboard combined with a pre-set rhythm/beat of your choice.

2. Use the other chord sequences to create other short pieces, possibly trying to combine them to form a longer one: you could experiment with different forms, such as ternary, rondo or arch-shape.

Performing activities

1. Work with others to perform your composition.

2. In a group, decide on one of the chord sequences and take turns to improvise over it while others play it.

   Try to record your performance so that you can listen to it and fully appreciate the different effects achieved.

QUESTION 32 0:00–0:41

This song was written for a film in 1957 for a film with the same name as the song. There have been countless covers of it including ones by José Carreras, a famous Spanish opera singer, and The Righteous Brothers, a very successful soul singing duo from the 1960s.

The excerpt will be played four times. You may find it helpful to tick a box each time you hear the excerpt.

☐ ☐ ☐ ☐

a. Name the melody instrument in this excerpt.

.... *(1 mark)*

b. Describe the accompaniment in the introduction.

....

....

(2 marks)

c. After the silent pause, how many non-pitched percussion instruments are playing? *Circle your answer.*

1   2   3   4

(1 mark)

d. There is one other instrument playing. What is it?

.... *(1 mark)*

e. What is the time signature of this excerpt?

.... *(1 mark)*

6

QUESTION 33   0:00–0:38

This excerpt combines the sounds of pitched and unpitched Indian instruments. The effect produced is quite unique and unmistakeable, and is also very colourful.

The excerpt will be played four times. You may find it helpful to tick a box each time you hear the excerpt.

☐ ☐ ☐ ☐

a. Name two of the instruments heard in this excerpt.

   i. ....

   ii. ....

(2 marks)

b. Describe the texture created by the two main melody instruments.

.... *(1 mark)*

c. Which **two** of the following techniques and devices can you hear in this excerpt? *Circle your choices.*

   augmentation   **ostinato**   **pitch bend**   **repetition**   **sequence**

(2 marks)

5

Composition activity

Compose a short piece of music for a solo instrument plus percussion accompaniment. Think carefully about your choices of timbre, rhythm, metre and melody.

Performing activity

Perform the composition written in response to the above stimulus and discuss the results with others in your group.

QUESTION 34   0:00–0:50

There is a mix of several traditions of music in this excerpt, a reflection of how the 20th and 21st centuries have moved on. The ease with which we can now travel around the world and share each other's cultures is a great opportunity. Enjoy it.

The excerpt will be played four times. You may find it helpful to tick a box each time you hear the excerpt.

☐ ☐ ☐ ☐

a. Which of the following melodic shapes represents the opening four notes?
Tick the correct one.

i. ☐

ii. ☐

iii. ☐

iv. ☐

(1 mark)

b. When this opening melodic shape is repeated in the next bar, how is it different?

....

(1 mark)

c. In the introduction you hear the words 'Takeova ENT' twice. What technical device is used on the second time you hear it?

....

(1 mark)

WORLD MUSIC

d. After this the main melody enters. It has four main phrases. Which **one** is very different from the other three? *Circle your answer.*

       first   **second**   **third**   **fourth**

(1 mark)

e. Which of the following statements describe this melody? Tick **two** boxes.

i. ☐ It moves mainly in steps.

ii. ☐ It moves mainly in leaps.

iii. ☐ It moves triadically.

iv. ☐ It moves chromatically.

v. ☐ There are repeated notes.

(2 marks)

6

Composing suggestion

If you have friends in the class who have knowledge and expertise in different musical cultures and traditions, share ideas and see if you can fuse the different styles into your compositions.

Listening activities

Find other examples of musical fusion. The Beatles were fond of this: listen to 'Love You To' and 'Norwegian Wood'. Rock 'n' roll is a fusion of two styles, as is punk rock.

Going further back, Mozart enjoyed the sounds of Turkey in his 'Rondo Alla Turca', while Debussy was captivated with the sound of the Indonesian gamelan and incorporated it into such pieces as *Pagodes*.

QUESTION 35 0:00–0:42

This excerpt features a wide variety of percussion instruments and was recorded live on location in Africa: it is easy to imagine a very atmospheric scene created by this dance music.

The excerpt will be played four times. You may find it helpful to tick a box each time you hear the excerpt.

☐ ☐ ☐ ☐

a. Which **two** of the following rhythmic devices can you can hear in the introduction to this excerpt? *Circle **two** choices.*

    augmentation   **diminution**   **dotted rhythms**

        ostinato   **regular rhythms**

(2 marks)

b. Which of the following best describes the form of this excerpt after the voices enter? *Circle your choice.*

    arch-shape   **binary**   **call-and-response**   **strophic**

(1 mark)

c. Describe the melody sung by the male voice in terms of range and techniques used.

....

....

....

(3 marks)

6

86   WORLD MUSIC

Composition activity

Use the rhythmic devices which are the correct answers to question (a) and the form/structure which is the correct answer to question (b) as the basis for a short composition. You can choose any instruments you wish.

Performing activities

1. Work with others to perform your composition.

2. As part of a group, perform music which uses the form/structure which is the correct answer to question (b) but is from other styles/genres.
Try to record your performances so that you can listen and fully appreciate the different effects.

QUESTION 36 0:00–1:07

This track comes from an album by Paul Simon called Graceland. *Much of it was recorded in South Africa when the country was ruled by an apartheid regime. By using many black South African musicians Paul Simon literally gave them a voice to speak out against oppression. He was also responsible for introducing the rest of the world to the now famous Ladysmith Black Mambazo vocal group, the singers on this track.*

The excerpt will be played four times. You may find it helpful to tick a box each time you hear the excerpt.

☐ ☐ ☐ ☐

a. Which of the following best describes the form or pattern of the opening? *Circle your answer.*

    binary   **call-and-response**   **ternary**

(1 mark)

b. What is the tonality of this music? *Circle your answer.*

    atonal   **major**   **minor**   **modal**

(1 mark)

c. Which of the following could be used to describe the second section (from the words 'Homeless')? *Circle **two** answers.*

    chromatic   **diatonic**   **homophonic**

    pentatonic   **polyphonic**

(2 marks)

4

Composing/Performing activities

1. Listen to the rest of this track and notice how the musicians create a 'symphonic' soundscape using only vocal sounds.

2. Each member of the class think of a vocal sound – it could be a hiss, a hum, a pop. There should be some long sounds, some short sounds, some high sounds, some low sounds, some loud sounds, some soft sounds. Share your sound with the rest of the class.

3. Choose some of the sounds to set up a pulse and a metre as the basis of the composition.

4. Any longer sounds can now be added to create a continuous 'wash' of musical colour.

5. The remaining sounds should be added in an improvisatory fashion to provide new interest.

6. Work out a structure, i.e. a beginning, a middle and an end. You might start with a loud explosive 'chord' with everyone calling out their sound together. You might start very quietly with only one sound and gradually layer the sounds on top of each other. If you need to have a director/conductor, take it in turns to do this.

Further listening

Ladysmith Black Mambazo are still going strong. Their album *Wenyukela* was recorded after the murder of the wife of the founder of the group, and is one of their most successful recent albums.

Listen to the track 'Music Has No Boundaries' from this album, and compare it with the track 'Homeless', which was recorded almost 20 years earlier. Write down similarities and differences in their style between these two tracks.

MOCK LISTENING EXAMINATIONS

In order to provide for teachers who wish to set a mock **Listening to and Appraising Music** examination for their pupils which matches the format of the final examination, we have chosen questions from each of the three **Strands of Learning** outlined in the AQA GCSE Music specification (see page 6 of this book).

This selection mixes questions from the three Strands, as will be the case in the final examination, and adds up to a total of 80 marks (all parts of a question are to be included, except where specified):

Question	Number of marks (Total: 80)
21	5
4	5
28	6
19	7
5(a)–(c) only	7
29	7
17(a)–(e) only	6
12	6
36	4
24	8
13	5
34	6
20	8

In addition, teachers may want to select questions for mini-examinations that concentrate on one of the three Strands of Learning. Here are our suggestions in each case:

THE WESTERN CLASSICAL TRADITION

Question	Number of marks (Total: 30)
1	5
4	5
12	6
5	9
13	5

POPULAR MUSIC OF THE 20TH AND 21ST CENTURIES

Question	Number of marks (Total: 35)
21	5
19	7
17	9
22	6
20	8

WORLD MUSIC

Question	Number of marks (Total: 30)
28	6
29	7
31	4
30	6
27	7

Of course, teachers should feel free to make their own selections of questions that best suit their particular needs, always checking the details of the specification to ensure as many of the **Areas of Study** (see pages 6 and 7–12 of this book) as possible are covered.

MOCK LISTENING EXAMINATIONS

GLOSSARY

Accelerando. Gradually getting faster.

Acciaccatura. A very short ornamental note (♪) played before a principal melodic note.

Allegro. A fast, lively tempo.

Alto. A low female voice or a countertenor.

Arch-shape or arch form. A symmetrical musical structure such as ternary form (ABA).

Atonal/atonal music. Music that is unrelated to a tonic note and therefore has no sense of key.

Augmentation. (1) (Usually) doubling the duration of each note of a rhythm or melody. (2) Extending the range of intervals upon repetition.

Barbershop choir. A specific style of a cappella (unaccompanied) singing by male or female voices, in four parts. The texture is mainly homophonic.

Bass. A low male voice.

Binary form. A musical structure in two sections (AB).

Boys' choir. A choir of boys' (treble) voices.

Brass quartet. A group of four brass players, usually two trumpets, a horn and a trombone, though other combinations are possible.

Broken chords. Spreading the notes of a chord.

Cadence. A point of repose at the end of a phrase, sometimes harmonised with two cadence chords. See **Imperfect cadence**, **Interrupted cadence**, **Perfect cadence** and **Plagal cadence**.

Call-and-response. A type of music in which a soloist sings or plays a phrase to which a larger group responds with an answering phrase.

Canon. A compositional device in which a melody in one part is repeated note for note in another part while the melody in the first part continues to unfold.

Chromatic. Where notes in the scale of the prevailing key are altered. An example would be G♯ in the scale of C major.

Clarinet quintet. Usually, a group of five players consisting of a clarinet and a string quartet. It can also be applied to an ensemble of five clarinet players (this would normally include a bass clarinet).

Con arco or **arco**. A direction to bow notes on a string instrument.

Countertenor. A male singer who uses falsetto.

Cross-rhythm. When one part has a rhythm that goes against the regular beat pattern (e.g. three triplet quavers against duplet quavers).

Diminution. (1) (Usually) halving the duration of notes in a melody or rhythm. (2) Reduction of the size of intervals upon repetition.

Distortion. Usually applied to guitar playing where a distorted sound is introduced by use of an amplifier or other electronic effect to alter the tone of the guitar.

Dominant. The fifth degree of a major or minor scale (e.g. G is the dominant of C).

Dotted rhythms. A rhythmic pattern which alternates dotted notes (notes whose value has been extended) with short notes, as in:

Drone. A continuous, sustained sound.

Drum fill or **fill**. A short passage played at the end of a musical phrase, improvising upon the prevailing rhythm. A fill can be played by any rock or pop instruments but usually refers to the drummer.

Echo. The effect of a delay long enough to produce a distinct copy of a sound.

Falsetto. A vocal technique which allows a man to sing higher notes (extending into the range of a female alto).

Finger-picking (or **fingerpicking**). The method of playing the guitar with one's fingertips, fingernails, or picks attached to fingers to pluck the strings.

Flute quartet. A chamber music group normally consisting of flute, violin, viola and cello; alternatively, it may refer to an ensemble of four flutes.

Glissando. A slide from one pitch to another.

Gospel choir. A choir which sings gospel music. The style is usually characterised by strong vocals, often harmonised, and lyrics of a usually Christian nature.

Ground bass. A melody in the bass that is repeated several times and which forms the basis for a continuous set of melodic and/or harmonic variations.

Hammer-on. U ly refers to the guitar-playing technique of bringing the fretting hand down strongly on the string just behind a fret, causing the string to sound.

Hemiola. A temporary change of metre from strong-weak-weak/strong-weak-weak (as in two bars of 3/4 time) to strong-weak/strong-weak/strong-weak (as in three bars of 2/4 time).

Imperfect cadence. An approach chord followed by chord V at the end of a phrase.

Interrupted cadence. Chord V followed by an unexpected chord (such as VI) at the end of a phrase.

Largo. A very slow tempo.

Lyrics. The text of a song.

Maestoso. Majestically.

Major. (1) A major interval is one semitone greater than a minor interval. The interval between C and E – the first three notes of a C major scale – is a major third – four semitones. (2) A major scale consists of eight different pitches rising stepwise by these intervals: tone–tone–semitone–tone–tone–tone–semitone.

Major 3rd. The interval between the first and third notes of a major scale, as in C up to E.

Major 6th. The interval between the first and sixth notes of a major scale, as in C up to A.

Major 7th. The interval between the first and seventh notes of a major scale, as in C up to B.

Male voice choir. A choir containing only male voices.

Minor. (1) A minor interval is one semitone less than a major interval. The interval between D and F – the first three notes of a D minor scale – is a minor third – three semitones. (2) A minor scale consists of eight different pitches rising stepwise by these intervals: tone–semitone–tone–tone–semitone–tone–tone. The seventh note is sometimes raised a semitone to form the leading note, thus giving rise to two forms of the minor scale: the harmonic and the melodic.

Mixed-voice choir. A choir containing both female and male voices.

Modal. Modal music is based on one of the scales of seven pitch classes commonly found in western music, but excluding the major and minor scales.

Moderato. A moderate tempo.

Ostinato. A rhythmic, harmonic or melodic pattern played many times in succession.

Pedal. A sustained or repeated note, usually but not necessarily in the bass, sounding against changing harmonies.

Pentatonic. Pentatonic music is based on a scale of five different pitches, such as C D F G A.

Perfect cadence. Chords V and I at the end of a phrase.

Perfect 4th. The interval between the first and fourth notes of a major or minor scale, as in C up to F.

Perfect 5th. The interval between the first and fifth notes of a major or minor scale, as in C up to G.

Piano quintet. A chamber music ensemble usually consisting of piano and a string quartet.

Pitch bend. Changing the pitch of a note by moving the string across the fret.

Plagal cadence. Chords IV and I at the end of a phrase.

Portamento. To slide between notes (similar to glissando).

Power chords. A term used by electric guitarists to refer to a chord that consists of just a root and a fifth. As there is no third, they are neither major nor minor, and are usually notated as 'open' when using chord symbols. For example, 'C open' means the notes C and G.

Presto. A very fast tempo.

Pull-off. Removing the finger from a vibrating string to produce a second pitch.

Repetition. In music, the restatement of a passage that has already been performed.

Riff. A short, catchy melodic figure, repeated like an **ostinato** and commonly found in rock, pop and jazz.

Scalic. An adjective referring to a melodic contour in which adjacent notes move by step in a similar manner to notes in a scale.

Sequence. The immediate repetition of a motif or phrase of a melody in the same part but at a different pitch. A harmonic progression can be treated in the same way.

Sequential. Phrases following one another as a **sequence**.

Soprano. The highest female voice.

String octet. Eight string players, comprising two string quartets (that is, four violins, two violas and two cellos).

Strophic. A strophic song is one where the same music is used for every verse (stanza) of the text.

Subdominant. The fourth degree of a major or minor scale (e.g. F in C major).

Submediant. The sixth degree of a scale.

Tenor. The highest naturally-produced male voice. (See **falsetto**.)

Ternary. In three parts. Ternary form is a three-part structure (ABA) in which the first and last sections are identical or very similar. These enclose a contrasting central section.

Time signature. Two numbers, one on top of the other, placed after the key signature at the beginning of a piece or section of a piece. The upper number indicates the number of beats per bar and the lower number indicates the time value of the beat.

Tonality. Music arranged wherein all the tones and semitones used relate to a tonic.

Tonic. The first degree of a major or minor scale.

Tremolo. The effect produced by the rapid repetition of a single note or alternation between two pitches.